The Compleat Bridge Player

The Compleat Bridge Player

VICTOR MOLLO

METHUEN

First published in Great Britain 1986
by Methuen London Ltd
11 New Fetter Lane, London EC4P 4EE

British Library Cataloguing in Publication Data

Mollo, Victor
    The compleat bridge player
    1. Contract bridge
    I. Title
    795.41'5   GV1282.3

ISBN 0-413-42290-9

Typeset by Words & Pictures Ltd
Thornton Heath, Surrey
Printed in Great Britain by
Richard Clay (The Chaucer Press) Ltd,
Bungay, Suffolk

Contents

Acknowledgments

As always, I am indebted to the American Contract Bridge League for its admirable handbooks on world events, and its daily *Bulletins* covering America's major tournaments.

Bridge d'Italia, *Le Bridgeur*, and José Le Dentu's column in *Le Figaro*, have again provided me with rich material.

This time I have had another source of inspiration — Giorgio Belladonna's *Dentro Bridge con Belladonna*, translated into French by Jean-Marc Roudinesco and Thierry Hugonet, and published by Pierre Belfond in two volumes, entitled respectively *Jouez au Bridge avec Belladonna* and *Le Bridge de Formule I*. It is a sad thought that this invaluable contribution to bridge literature hasn't, so far, been translated into English.

For the twenty-ninth time — for unless I have miscounted this is my twenty-ninth book — I am deeply grateful to my wife, the Squirrel. Never has an erring husband been forgiven so often. Again and again, she has found me out attributing the ◊6 to North and East, without giving either the ◊3 or ◊4; or else I have presented South and West alike with the ♠5, allowing neither the ♠6 or ♠7. In the good old days it was enough to put x's for all cards below honour rank. The great Ewart Kempson taught me the virtues of designating each pygmy separately. I approve of virtue, so long as it doesn't call for constancy. Of that I am not capable. But I have learned to be forgiven for my sins, so if you spot some hitherto un-noted peccadillo, please don't tell anyone, more especially the Squirrel, who might take it personally.

Preface

The time-honoured approach to bridge is strictly objective. No personal considerations cloud the issue. What's right for George is right for Harry. In taking a simple finesse, as in executing a complex squeeze, Jane and Joan apply the same technique for there is no other. That is sound enough as far as it goes. The trouble is that it doesn't go far enough.

The approach in these pages will be largely subjective. I have discovered no new stratagems or manoeuvres, but I have looked at one and all from the viewpoint of the player holding the cards. When the cardinal points come to life and blood runs through their veins, it is no longer true that Harry and George, Jane and Joan, play the same way in identical situations. Once we leave the elementary mechanics behind, their paths diverge. It cannot be otherwise, for George is by nature a pragmatist, Harry a theoretician; Jane is bold, Joan is cautious. Some children at school study the classics, others science. When they grow up they will not respond to the problems they face in like manner.

In the pages to come I propose to examine the skills that make up the art of bridge, isolate and identify each one in turn, and allow the reader to recognise where lies his weakness and where his strength, to correct the one and to nourish the other, to find himself, as it were, in the scheme of things and so realise his full potential. He owes no less to his ego, and whether we like it or not, the irresistible fascination of bridge is that it allows the ego — foibles, follies and all — the fullest expression.

A question arises: how well *should* you play?

The answer, far from obvious, depends on your objective. If it's winning, it doesn't call for skill so much as finding the right milieu, where you play better than the others. If you want to improve, the opposite applies. Play with your betters and lose. Winning will boost your ego in one way, improving your game in another. But winning and playing well alike are only the means to the end, which is to derive from the greatest game in the world the greatest pleasures it has to offer. Just how much skill that requires depends on each individual in turn.

You may end up playing *too* well. Just as a girl may be too beautiful if she keeps her looks by rigorous dieting, privations, early hours – in short, a misspent youth – so the price of expertise may be too high, especially if it means going the full distance.

Learning, improving, climbing up the ladder is exciting and brings with it a sense of achievement. But you don't have to get to the top if it makes you dizzy. The journey is more enjoyable than the arrival.

Having warned you against the perils of striving for the top, I feel free to point the way. After all, you can break off the journey at any stage if it's too fatiguing.

In this book there is nothing for the beginner, but with copious illustrations from the summit and from the big money game alike, the reader will see bridge in every form. He will learn something from the brilliance of the masters and more from their lapses, for he will see what causes them, not shortcomings in technique, but personality faults, lack of self-discipline, an uneven temperament, failure to respond to the vibrations round the table. Approaching each theme subjectively, he will learn more about himself – and there he will find the key both to playing better and, more important, to enjoying the game more than he does already.

On the shores of the Lake of Eternal Life in Shangri La, screened from the sun by a canopy of azure clouds, stands the Temple of the Compleat Bridge Player. In its lofty halls and spacious galleries the visitor will meet *homo sapiens* at bridge, at turns wise and foolish, grave and comic, subtle and simple. As he bids and plays, his ego comes through to reveal the inner man, for at bridge no artist can fail to betray his true nature. As the spotlight shifts from one human trait to another, the visitor will see how the springs are set in motion, his own as well as those of masters of legendary fame, for shorn of the outsize fig leaves which protect him in the world at large, his ego too will be exposed.

Inspired by the inscription on Apollo's statue at Delphi, the words on the golden gates at the entrance to the Temple are: Know Thyself.

CHAPTER ONE

Technique: what is it?

Meet the technician. He knows what to do, though not always what makes him do it. No introspective Hamlet, he neither needs, nor desires, to analyse his mental processes.

Among the upper crust a high level of technique is taken for granted. But what exactly is it? To view the picture in perspective it must be mounted in the right frame.

In all its forms and at every stage, from the primitive to the most advanced, technique is divorced from the personal factor which dominates every other aspect of bridge. Psychology doesn't come into it. The ego, clamouring for self-expression at all other times, is kept in a strait-jacket. Greed, cunning, daring play no part. Each problem must be solved within its own dimension, the cardinal points remaining disembodied throughout. This isn't always apparent at the card table, when technical considerations are often interlocked with others.

An anatomy of technique would take us through three main stages. The first consists of the bare mechanics. The next is intelligent anticipation. Every move in bidding and in play, in attack as in defence, must be prepared for those that are likely to follow. This is the one salient feature which bridge has in common with chess.

The third stage is experience. Often enough, the expert doesn't, indeed, cannot, foresee how a hand will develop, but he has learned to take precautions and to envisage possibilities, good and bad, of which the novice is unaware. He lacks the ringcraft.

It will be rewarding to go through each stage in turn, starting at the bottom and climbing, rung by rung, to the top of the ladder.

THE MECHANICS

Safety plays, which remain the same regardless of who sits where, provide a perfect background for a study of technique in isolation.

We'll start with the simplest and best known of all:

$$\text{AQ1065} \qquad\qquad \text{7432}$$

This is the trump suit in a small slam. With entries in plenty and no outside losers, how do you handle the trumps?

Even if you had never come across this situation before, in print if not at the table, you would soon work out what to do. It's the reasoning that leads to the correct play that is instructive, for it provides the matrix for many far more complex situations.

Your first idea would be to finesse twice. Good odds, for you would only lose to the bare KJ over you. A second look would tell you that you can do better still by laying down the ace first. You may drop a singleton king, a chance to nothing, and your contract would still be safe against any other trump break — except KJx(x) over you, and for that there's no remedy. It is true that if the king is under your AQ your play may cost a trick, but obviously you will be paying a small premium on a big policy.

You solved the problem in two stages. First you identified the threat, a bare KJ over you. Then you found the way to parry it by laying down the ace.

Let's apply the same process in a less obvious situation.

♠ K J 7 5		♠ A Q 10 8 4 2
♡ A 9 2	N	♡ 5
◇ A Q 6 5	W E	◇ J 7 3 2
♣ A K	S	♣ 6 3

At favourable vulnerability, North passes and after an uncontested auction you reach 6♠. North leads the ♣J. On the ♠A he discards a club.

Can you make reasonably certain of the contract? The problem is posed in an article by French international Philippe Cronier.

Clearly your only danger is a bad diamond break. So you start by eliminating the side-suits. The ♡A and a heart ruff are followed by a trump to hand and another heart ruff. A third trump and the ♣A(K) now set the stage.

You can guard against any diamond break, providing that you know who has the length. Here it can only be North, who has a void in spades. With twelve or thirteen cards in hearts and clubs he might have said something. So you lead the ◇5 to dummy's knave and duck a second diamond on the way back. North must lead into your ◇AQ or present you with a ruff and discard.

If you suspected South of being long in diamonds, it would make no difference. You would finesse the ◇Q first, then duck.

Again, you have identified the danger, then parried it. The next case may require a little more care. The hand came up in the BBC's third Grand Slam TV series.

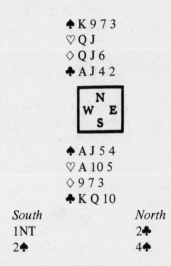

♠ K 9 7 3
♡ Q J
◇ Q J 6
♣ A J 4 2

♠ A J 5 4
♡ A 10 5
◇ 9 7 3
♣ K Q 10

South	North
1NT	2♣
2♠	4♠

I was South. Jane Priday, West, began with the ◇K, ◇A and a third diamond. No ruff. A good start to what looked like a text-book hand. Before drawing trumps I take the heart finesse. If it succeeds, I can afford a safety play — first the ♠A, then a low trump, inserting the ♠9, so ensuring my contract against a 4–1 break.

When the finesse failed and Jane returned another heart, I could afford no safety plays. The ♠Q had to be right and that's all there was to it. So I laid down the ♠K and . . .

Grinning broadly, Tony Priday dropped his bare queen. This was the deal:

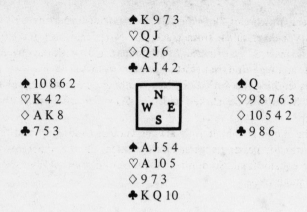

♠ K 9 7 3
♡ Q J
◇ Q J 6
♣ A J 4 2

♠ 10 8 6 2
♡ K 4 2
◇ A K 8
♣ 7 5 3

♠ Q
♡ 9 8 7 6 3
◇ 10 5 4 2
♣ 9 8 6

♠ A J 5 4
♡ A 10 5
◇ 9 7 3
♣ K Q 10

My bad play is instructive, as bad plays so often are. Having identified the main problem I assumed that there would be no other. It was right to take the heart finesse first, and when it failed, to play for the spade finesse to succeed. But to start with the ♠K was bad technique. Since I didn't have the ♠8, bringing down West's bare queen wouldn't have helped me. I should have led a low spade from dummy. That could gain, as above, and couldn't lose.

It was bad luck — on Irving Rose who was my partner.

TIMING

This time you are West.

♠ 6 3
♡ A Q
◇ A K J 9 6 4
♣ K 5 2

♠ A K J 10
♡ 10 6
◇ 7 5 3 2
♣ A Q J

North leads a club against 6◇. You lay down the ◇A and South shows out. Can you make certain of the contract regardless of the distribution?

It looks easy. You cash the ◇K and your top winners, except, of course, the ♡A, and you throw North in with a trump, presenting him with three different ways of committing hara-kiri. He can return a club, giving you a ruff and discard, a heart into your AQ; or a spade, setting up a trick for you whoever has the queen.

And yet, if you play as thoughtlessly as I did on the last hand, you can go down. It all depends on the order in which you cashed your winners. Which card did you play at trick four, after the ◇K? A club? Then you have fallen from grace, for North may ruff and exit safely with a spade. If you finesse, South may turn up with the queen. If you don't, you may find that North started with Qxxx.

Try cashing the ♠AK first. Now nothing can go wrong, for if North ruffs, South will be marked with the ♠Q and a ruffing finesse will pick her up.

The moral is that it isn't always enough to identify and parry the main threat. Lesser dangers, lurking unseen in the undergrowth, may prove equally fatal. So don't be lulled into a sense of false security till the hand is over.

LOOKING AHEAD

To change the scenery the reader will be South this time in a match-pointed pairs event, where that extra trick is so important, especially when it looks as if the whole field will be in the same contract. Here it is 6NT, reached after an uncontested auction.

♠ A 10 2
♡ K Q
◇ A 10 5
♣ A Q 9 5 4

♠ K J 9 8 3
♡ A 9 4
◇ Q J
♣ K 6 3

You win the heart lead with the king and at once your thoughts turn to the spades. You can finesse either way, but you can only pick up a well-guarded queen if East, not West, is the culprit. So you start with the ♠A and run the ♠10. It holds, West following. Now you have twelve certain tricks, but for a good score you need thirteen. So what is your next move?

Perhaps you didn't think the order of play to be particularly important, and doing what comes naturally, cashed the spades. If so, what did you throw from dummy? Presumably, two diamonds, for you will have to find another discard on the ♡A and you expect a long club in dummy to yield the thirteenth trick. Look at the four hands and you will soon see where you went wrong.

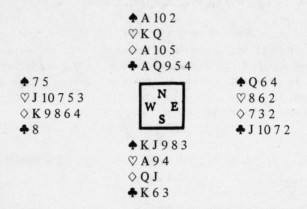

The clubs break 4–1, and to compensate for this piece of bad luck you need the diamond finesse. It's right, but, alas, you have bared the ◇A and can no longer take it.

It was your lack of technique — failure to think ahead — that brought about your undoing. At trick three, as soon as the ♠10 held, you should have tested the clubs. Seeing West show out you would have known that you needed the diamond finesse and played accordingly.

We will give this hand another twist. Suppose that you suspected East of having the ◇K. Perhaps he doubled a cue-bid in diamonds or maybe he showed an exaggerated interest in the bidding. No longer need you pin your hopes on the finesse. Finding that he has four clubs, you can subject him to a squeeze in the minors, but this again calls for forethought — in other words, for more technique.

To set the stage for the 3-card ending, you must play off the ♡Q and lay down the ◇A, the key move. Now, having unblocked, you are free to discard dummy's two diamonds on the spades, leaving ♣Q9 as the last two cards. Your own will be ◇Q ♣6. Turn to East, assuming that he started with the ◇K. Your last winner forces him to part with a card from ◇K ♣J10.

The mental process behind the unblocking play — the *Vienna Coup* — is the same as in the case of the straightforward finesse. Declarer looks ahead, envisages the dangers and sets out to counter them in good time.

This hand came up in the North American Spring Nationals in Montreal in 1985.

EXPERIENCE

The way to stardom can be greatly shortened by reading books and learned treatises, but there's no substitute for experience. Just as so many plays have been standardised, so have many other manoeuvres. To do the right thing the technician doesn't have to start from first principles. Having been there so often before, the correct approach becomes second nature.

A flashback to the early days of bridge may surprise those of us who take our present level of technique for granted. Our ancestors could play extremely well, yet on occasion they perpetrated blunders which wouldn't be seen in good company today. We have learned a lot from past mistakes.

A fascinating example goes back to the first international match between Britain and America, played at Selfridges in London in 1933.

Love all: dealer North

♠ A K J 10 8 6
♡ 6 4
◇ K 4
♣ K 7 2

```
    N
  W   E
    S
```

♠ None
♡ A K Q J 10 7 5
◇ A J 8 7 6
♣ 8

South	West	North	East
—	—	1♠	Pass
3♡	Pass	3♠	Pass
4◇	Pass	4♠	Pass
5♡	Pass	5♠	Pass
6♡			

The bidding is gauche, to say the least, but the slam is a good one and was reached in both rooms, with Josephine Culbertson — after the above sequence — as declarer for the Americans, and Colonel Beasley for the British.

Both Wests led the ♣Q and both Souths played throughout in identical fashion. Assuming a club continuation, how would you set about it?

Strange to relate, both Souths went up with dummy's ♣K, losing to the ace. Ruffing the next club, they laid down the ♡A and went over to the ◇K to throw two diamonds on the ♠AK. Next they played the ◇A and a third diamond. West ruffed with the ♡8 in front of dummy and that was that. Flat board!

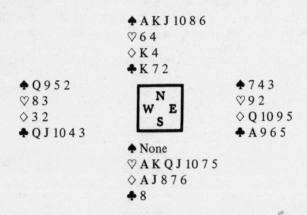

♠ A K J 10 8 6
♡ 6 4
◇ K 4
♣ K 7 2

♠ Q 9 5 2   ♠ 7 4 3
♡ 8 3   ♡ 9 2
◇ 3 2   ◇ Q 10 9 5
♣ Q J 10 4 3   ♣ A 9 6 5

♠ None
♡ A K Q J 10 7 5
◇ A J 8 7 6
♣ 8

A deplorable lack of technique all round. The attempt to ruff the third diamond showed an unfamiliarity with the odds which you wouldn't find today in far less exalted circles. The straightforward finesse is an even-money chance, a 3-3 split is 2-1 against. We all know it, not because we are gifted mathematicians, but because we have met this situation and read about it more often than we can remember. Josephine Culbertson and Colonel Beasley must have known the odds, at least in theory, but they hadn't become a part of their everyday lives.

No less culpable than the attempted ruff was the thoughtless play of the ♣K at trick one. It couldn't possibly gain. Why, then, did two of the best players of the day do it? Because they couldn't see the purpose of retaining the ♣K in dummy. Squeezes were not as common then as they are now and the value of the ♣K as a menace wasn't apparent.

To the technician the hand presents no serious problem. He ducks the first club, ruffs the next one and reels off six more trumps, coming to this 6-card ending.

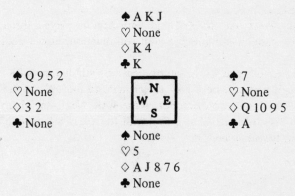

```
              ♠ A K J
              ♡ None
              ◇ K 4
              ♣ K
♠ Q 9 5 2                      ♠ 7
♡ None          N              ♡ None
◇ 3 2        W     E           ◇ Q 10 9 5
♣ None          S              ♣ A
              ♠ None
              ♡ 5
              ◇ A J 8 7 6
              ♣ None
```

On the last trump East parts with a diamond, but what can he throw on the second spade? Having to keep the ♣A, he is forced to bare the ◇Q. Had West the ◇Q he would have been squeezed in spades and diamonds.

Just as the technician knows how to handle different card combinations according to the odds, so he is always alive to the possibility of subjecting either defender, or both, to a squeeze. His own experience and that of others, conveyed by word of mouth and through countless diagrams in print, have taught him the deadly effect of piling on the pressure.

We are back in modern times with all the mistakes of the past to draw upon:

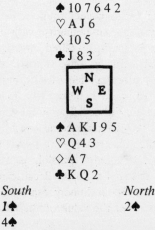

```
              ♠ 10 7 6 4 2
              ♡ A J 6
              ◇ 10 5
              ♣ J 8 3
                  N
               W     E
                  S
              ♠ A K J 9 5
              ♡ Q 4 3
              ◇ A 7
              ♣ K Q 2
```

South	*North*
1♠	2♠
4♠	

West leads the ♦Q. What should be South's plan? Yes, of course West has the three missing trumps or there would be no story to tell. Likewise, he must have the ♡K or it wouldn't have a happy ending.

When you have made the first two moves, I'll tell you what happened. Ready?

South saw at once that his only hope was an end-play against West, much on the lines of the deal on page 4. So he set out to strip the hand, beginning with the ♣K. East won and returned the ♡9 to dummy's ♡J. After cashing the clubs declarer played the ♠K – the ♠A had gone – and another spade, throwing West in. A diamond to East's king and another heart set up the fourth, lethal trick for the defence.

Can you see where South went wrong?

A technician would never have allowed the defenders to play so well.

To stop them required no coup or savant manoeuvre, just an elementary precaution – allowing West's ♦Q to hold at trick one. Thereafter all the moves would have been the same, with this vital difference, that when West was thrown in with the ♠Q he would not have had a safe exit, for now a diamond would present declarer with a ruff and discard.

Should South have foreseen all this at trick one? Theoretically, perhaps, but in practice the game would become infinitely slow and tedious if players tried to look too far ahead, allowing for all the possible permutations. Most of the time it isn't necessary.

The technician ducks the ♦Q, not because he can see the future, but because he has observed in the past how desirable it is to cut enemy communications. He must lose a diamond anyway. If he wins the first one defenders can decide which of them will come on play with the second. If the ♦A is held up they are denied this option.

This time experience will come to our aid in defence. The hand occurred in an inter-club match in France.

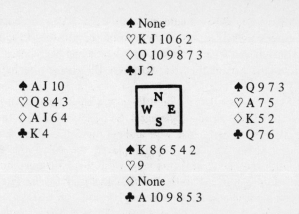

♠ None
♡ K J 10 6 2
◇ Q 10 9 8 7 3
♣ J 2

♠ A J 10
♡ Q 8 4 3
◇ A J 6 4
♣ K 4

♠ Q 9 7 3
♡ A 7 5
◇ K 5 2
♣ Q 7 6

♠ K 8 6 5 4 2
♡ 9
◇ None
♣ A 10 9 8 5 3

After a 1◇ opening by West, East became declarer in 3NT. South, who had overcalled East's 1♠ response with 2♣, led the ♣10. Declarer went up with dummy's ♣K — North jettisoning the knave to unblock — and came to hand with the ◇K. The ♠Q followed, then the ♠7 to the ♠J and the ♠A, East throwing his ♠9.

At trick six East returned to hand with the ♡A, but by now the fate of the hand had been sealed. If South still had the ♠2 declarer could be kept to eight tricks. If he had let that precious card go, he couldn't be denied a ninth.

Observe what happens if, after the ♡A, East leads the ♠3 and is left on play! Dummy's ◇A will be his only other trick. Suppose, however, that having parted with the ♠2, South has to overtake. He can cash two more spades and the ♣A, but his next card, inevitably a club, will not only present declarer with a trick — making up for the fourth spade — but will also force North to unguard one of the red suits.

This is how the hand was actually played. South retained the ♠2 and so defeated the contract.

When North showed out in spades and South in diamonds, declarer could play double-dummy, but how did South come to guard so jealously his ♠2? Could he, at tricks three and four, foresee so clearly the end-position? Of course not, but being an experienced player, he knew the importance of the lowest card in the pack. With it he could decide whether to win a trick or to lose it. Without it he would have no option. As in the previous hand, technique was born of experience.

A little technique could have averted a lot of bad luck here. Against
6♠ West led the 4♠.

♠ A 8 3
♡ 5
◇ A Q 6 4 2
♣ K 8 5 2

♠ K Q J 2
♡ A 8 6 4 2
◇ K 3
♣ A 7

South could see ten top tricks and set out to get two more by ruffing
hearts in dummy. Unfortunately East over-ruffed the second time and
the hand collapsed. Declarer consoled himself with the reflection that
a 5-2 break is only a 30 per cent chance, so seven times out of ten his
play would have succeeded. Besides, what else could he do?

The correct technique is to duck in diamonds at trick two, the ◇2
from dummy, the ◇3 from hand. Whatever the return − another trump
is best − South cashes the ♡A, ruffs a heart and scores twelve tricks
with: four spades, four diamonds, two clubs, the ♡A and a heart ruff.
This simple line of play allows for the likely 4-2 breaks in spades
and diamonds, as was the case:

♠ A 8 3
♡ 5
◇ A Q 6 4 2
♣ K 8 5 2

♠ 10 6 5 4   ♠ 9 7
♡ K J 9 7 3   ♡ Q 10
◇ 10 8   ◇ J 9 7 5
♣ J 9   ♣ Q 10 6 4 3

♠ K Q J 2
♡ A 8 6 4 2
◇ K 3
♣ A 7

Why did declarer go wrong? Probably because ruffing is part of the elementary mechanics. Ducking in a suit with all the tops requires a little technique.

A little more is required on the hand below, or maybe it's a case of advanced common sense — which is the same thing.

ADVANCED COMMONSENSE

South is American champion, Paul Soloway, playing against Germany in the 1984 Olympiad in Seattle. After a double from West of the 1◇ opening, North–South reach 3NT.

Both vul: dealer South

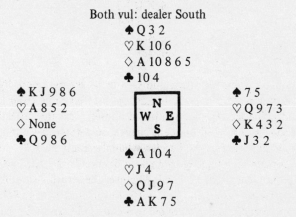

```
              ♠ Q 3 2
              ♡ K 10 6
              ◇ A 10 8 6 5
              ♣ 10 4

♠ K J 9 8 6              ♠ 7 5
♡ A 8 5 2        N       ♡ Q 9 7 3
◇ None        W     E    ◇ K 4 3 2
♣ Q 9 8 6        S       ♣ J 3 2

              ♠ A 10 4
              ♡ J 4
              ◇ Q J 9 7
              ♣ A K 7 5
```

West leads a low spade, declarer's ♠10 winning. How should he continue? If the diamond finesse succeeds South has ten top tricks. If it fails the ♡K could provide the ninth. An excellent contract.

"A difficult hand, brilliant play," said the daily *Bulletin*. I thought the praise overdone — until I tried the hand out on some very fair players. All started with the diamond finesse — uninspired, to say the least.

If the finesse loses, as above, a spade through the closed hand will set up three winners for West and it will then be too late to find the ♡A in the right place. Anticipating this position at trick two, Paul Soloway led the ♡4, rising with dummy's king when West played low. Now he could afford to get back with a club and take the diamond finesse in safety.

Needless to say, it wouldn't have helped West to go up with the ♡A for he couldn't lead a spade profitably from his side.

TALENT

A mastery of the mechanics and experience, two of the basic ingredients which make up technique, can both be acquired — the former through study, the latter with patience. The third factor, forethought, can, it is true, be developed but it requires talent and that isn't given to everyone.

Analysis will often show that a player's talent can be measured in tricks — not the number he makes, but the number he sees ahead. In good company everyone is familiar with all the high-sounding coups and the classical *modus operandi*, but not everyone can set the stage at trick one for the coup to come at trick four.

This is a hand from the Montreal Nationals in 1985.

```
       ♠ Q 10 6
       ♡ A K J
       ◇ A 8 7 5
       ♣ 9 6 3

            N
        W       E
            S

       ♠ K J 9 8 4 3 2
       ♡ None
       ◇ K J 10
       ♣ K J 2
```

After a highly competitive auction, in which West overcalled in hearts and was supported by East, South became declarer in 5♠. West led the ◇9.

How do you set about making eleven tricks, or rather preventing opponents from scoring three?

Messieurs, faites vos jeux. Rien ne va plus.

Which card did you play at trick two? The contract depends on it. If you ran the opening lead up to your hand, the 'natural' thing to do, you will be unlucky, and deservedly so, for West will rise with the ♠A, put East in with the ♣A and ruff a diamond.

The sight of the ◇9, an obvious singleton, should have sounded the toxin. Joe Steponavic, declarer, heard it loud and clear. To parry the threat he rose with the ◇A and took three rounds of hearts, discarding his ♣KJ2. This was the deal:

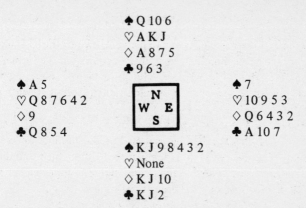

♠ Q 10 6
♡ A K J
◇ A 8 7 5
♣ 9 6 3

♠ A 5
♡ Q 8 7 6 4 2
◇ 9
♣ Q 8 5 4

♠ 7
♡ 10 9 5 3
◇ Q 6 4 3 2
♣ A 10 7

♠ K J 9 8 4 3 2
♡ None
◇ K J 10
♣ K J 2

The defence scored a trick in hearts to which they had no right, instead of the ♣A to which they were entitled, but now West had no way of putting East in to give him a ruff. Communications had been snipped — by the *Scissors Coup*.

The mechanics of the coup present no mystery. It's in seeing the need for it before playing to the first trick that declarer showed his mettle.

Looking ahead remains the motif on the next hand, but this time you are West.

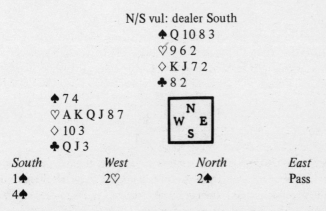

N/S vul: dealer South

♠ Q 10 8 3
♡ 9 6 2
◇ K J 7 2
♣ 8 2

♠ 7 4
♡ A K Q J 8 7
◇ 10 3
♣ Q J 3

South	West	North	East
1♠	2♡	2♠	Pass
4♠			

On your ♡K East plays the ♡5 and South the ♡4. The ♡3 is missing, so clearly both East and South started with doubletons. How do you visualise the defence? Do you cash the ♡A and switch in the ♣Q, hoping to score a trick in each minor? Or do you play a third round of hearts?

One or the other would be the line adopted by most defenders. Derek Rimington, who was West, did neither. After the ♡K he switched at once to the ♣Q. Why? Because he could see that unless South, marked on the bidding with both minor suit aces, had three diamonds, there was no hope. The defence could only succeed if he had three diamonds and ♣Ax, in which case cashing the ♡A could be fatal. South would draw trumps, ruff dummy's third heart, cash the ♣A and exit with a club, forcing the defence to open up the diamonds, or concede a ruff and discard. This was the deal which came up in the Caransa tournament in Amsterdam in 1978.

                 ♠ Q 10 8 3
                 ♡ 9 6 2
                 ◇ K J 7 2
                 ♣ 8 2

♠ 7 4   ♠ 6
♡ A K Q J 8 7   ♡ 5 3
◇ 10 3   ◇ Q 6 5 4
♣ Q J 3   ♣ K 10 9 7 6 5

                 ♠ A K J 9 5 2
                 ♡ 10 4
                 ◇ A 9 8
                 ♣ A 4

The switch to the ♣Q at trick two prevented declarer from eliminating, for having taken their trick in clubs, defenders could *exit* safely in hearts.

    Observe that if either East or West broaches the diamonds, declarer can hardly go wrong.

THE EGO RECTIFIES THE COUNT

Before concluding this chapter I have a confession to make. I stated categorically on the first page: 'In all its forms technique is divorced from the personal factor.' That is an over-simplification. It is true that technique involves no psychology. Safety plays, squeezes, uppercuts, *Merrimac* and *Deschapelles Coups* function alike regardless of who is at the table. And yet even from the routine mechanics of the game the ego cannot be excluded. So let me rectify the count.

    Faced with the choice between a finesse and a squeeze, the more ambitious players will rely on the squeeze, not because it offers better odds — they are assumed to be the same — but because anyone can take a finesse, whereas a squeeze calls for a measure of sophistication. Some players, especially young ones, will on occasion accept inferior odds, regarding finesses as being undignified. Pride bends the odds.

Mathematicians are likewise apt to over-indulge their egos. Players and writers, too, for that matter, will work out the odds for or against a particular line of play to the nearest percentage point.

I deplore this practice. For one thing I don't believe that odds of 2 or 3 per cent exist at bridge. A cough, a sneeze, the time it takes an opponent to play to a trick, his air of contentment or dejection, all are worth more.

No less important is the waste of mental effort. Concentration is a vital factor and if a player expends his energy on trivia he will be less able to concentrate on the things that matter.

Subject to these reservations, technique belongs to the realms of science in which the personal equation has no place.

A knowledge of the mechanics will suffice to put a player in a commanding position in the post-mortem. To become a member of the upper crust calls for more, much more. Resilience, imagination, occasional flashes of inspiration, these are the hallmarks of quality. And this transcends the realms of science.

CHAPTER TWO

Mind over Matter

As we leave the Hall of Science and ascend the broad marble staircase, past the busts of Aristotle and Hippocrates, Newton and Einstein, we see waiting to greet us at the top, East and West, North and South — but no longer are they the dessicated cardinal points we left behind. Rosy-cheeked, pulsating with life, they are human, just as we are. Their thoughts and emotions are the same as ours. They hope, they fear, they are clever, sometimes too clever. They plot, they scheme, they set traps, and sometimes they fall into them.

In seeking to overcome them it isn't enough to read their cards. We must also probe their intentions. Technique will help us up to a point. Beyond that, psychology should be our guide.

Sitting South you hold Bobby Wolff's cards in a preliminary round against France during the 1971 World Championship at Taipeh.

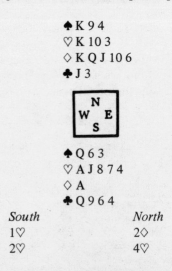

♠ K 9 4
♡ K 10 3
◇ K Q J 10 6
♣ J 3

```
   N
 W   E
   S
```

♠ Q 6 3
♡ A J 8 7 4
◇ A
♣ Q 9 6 4

South	North
1♡	2◇
2♡	4♡

Henri Svarc, West, leads the ♣5. Jean-Michel Boulenger goes up with the ♣A and returns the ♣2. Svarc wins with the ♠A, cashes the ♣K and exits with a low spade.

How would you continue?

Bobby Wolff reflected: rising with the ♠A was surely an unnatural play. Why was Svarc in such a hurry to cash his winners? The only rational explanation is that he expected a trick in trumps to set the contract. Bobby played accordingly. Winning the spade return in hand, he led the ♡J, covered by Svarc with the ♡Q and won in dummy. Back in hand with the ◇A, Bobby Wolff led the ♡8, finessing against the ♡9.

This was the complete deal:

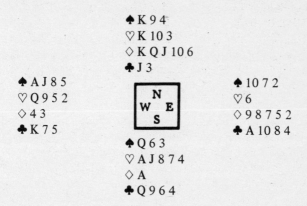

```
                    ♠ K 9 4
                    ♡ K 10 3
                    ◇ K Q J 10 6
                    ♣ J 3
  ♠ A J 8 5                              ♠ 10 7 2
  ♡ Q 9 5 2          N                   ♡ 6
  ◇ 4 3           W     E                ◇ 9 8 7 5 2
  ♣ K 7 5            S                   ♣ A 10 8 4
                    ♠ Q 6 3
                    ♡ A J 8 7 4
                    ◇ A
                    ♣ Q 9 6 4
```

Technique by itself wouldn't have brought home the contract, which failed in the other room.

Following the same processes as passed through Bobby Wolff's mind in Taipeh, take Fritzi Gordon's hand at the European Championships in Warsaw, in 1966, during the crucial match with Italy.

Fritzi Gordon   *Rixi Markus*
♠ Q 8 7 5   ♠ A K 10 2
♡ A Q 4   ♡ 8 6
◇ J 4 2   ◇ 10 5
♣ A 9 6   ♣ K J 10 7 3

West	North	East	South
—	—	1♣	1◇
1♠	2◇	2♠	Pass
3◇	Pass	3♠	Pass
4♠			

The bidding was straightforward. Fritzi's 3◇ over Rixi's simple raise was exploratory, leaving the way open for 3NT if it should suit partner, who might have had three spades only.

North led a low diamond to partner's king. On the ◇A, which followed, Fritzi threw the knave and North the queen, an unmistakable suit preference signal. East duly switched to a heart, the queen losing to the king. At trick four North played a diamond.

Why? Didn't he believe Fritzi's ◇J? He had no reason to doubt it, and unless it was a false card it would present Fritzi with a ruff and discard. Only a holding of four trumps to the knave could explain such magnanimity. Intercepting North's thoughts, Fritzi ruffed, leaving dummy with ♠AK10, cashed the ♠A and came to hand with the ♡A to finesse the ♠10.

When South showed out, it only remained to make the right guess in clubs. Game, set and match, and the Women's European title for Britain.

YOU'RE NOT INFALLIBLE?
NEITHER ARE THEY

Even the best opponents should be given the chance to err. The second best should be led into temptation at every turn. We'll start with a primitive example to build on for the more subtle ones to follow.

How do you set about making 6♠ as West?

♠ K J 10 7 5		♠ A Q
♡ A K J	**N** **W E** **S**	♡ 7 4 3 2
◇ A Q 6		◇ 9
♣ 9 2		♣ A Q 8 5 4 3

North leads a trump. If the diamond finesse wins you can ruff a diamond and bring the slam home with one of two finesses, hearts or clubs. It's a tall order. A more promising line of play is to draw trumps, duck a club, then finesse the ♣Q.

To improve your chances play a low club from dummy at trick two. Few Souths, holding ♣Kx, would fail to go up with the king. Then you might make the contract even against an unfavourable distribution. This won't work against an expert South, who would quickly return another club, cutting a vital link between declarer and dummy. But then not all defenders are experts and even experts have been known to fall from grace — except at the inquest.

Here, in a pairs event at Juan-les-Pins, we have an all-star cast.

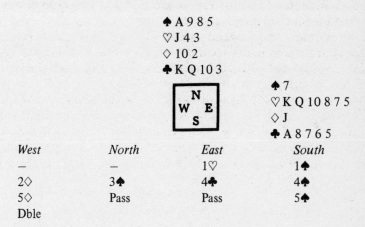

♠ A 9 8 5
♡ J 4 3
◇ 10 2
♣ K Q 10 3

♠ 7
♡ K Q 10 8 7 5
◇ J
♣ A 8 7 6 5

West	North	East	South
—	—	1♡	1♠
2◇	3♣	4♣	4♠
5◇	Pass	Pass	5♠
Dble			

You are Walter Avarelli, sitting East. Camillo Pabis-Ticci, West, leads the ◇A, the ◇K and then the ♣4. Dummy's card is the ♣3. How do you defend?

Avarelli won with the ♣A and played back another club for Pabis-Ticci to ruff.

These were the four hands:

♠ A 9 8 5
♡ J 4 3
◇ 10 2
♣ K Q 10 3

♠ 4 3
♡ None
◇ A K Q 9 7 6 5 3
♣ J 9 4

♠ 7
♡ K Q 10 8 7 5
◇ J
♣ A 8 7 6 5

♠ K Q J 10 6 2
♡ A 9 6 2
◇ 8 4
♣ 2

Bob Slavenberg, South, promptly discarded a heart and later two more hearts on dummy's ♣KQ10. Only one down and a pretty cold bottom for the Italians.

Slavenberg's play of the ♣3 from dummy was, of course, more

subtle than declarer's play on the previous hand, but basically it was the same manoeuvre — putting an opponent to a guess and so giving him a chance to misguess.

Giorgio Belladonna points out that Pabis-Ticci was at fault for playing the ◊K at trick two. Had he led the ◊Q, denying the king, Avarelli would have ruffed and given Pabis-Ticci a heart ruff. A club to the ace, the ♡Q, now master, and a second heart ruff would have set the contract by four tricks, enough to win the tournament. Even experts . . .

This time you are declarer:

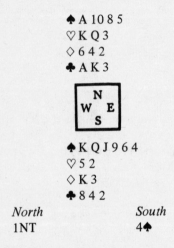

♠ A 10 8 5
♡ K Q 3
◊ 6 4 2
♣ A K 3

♠ K Q J 9 6 4
♡ 5 2
◊ K 3
♣ 8 4 2

North	South
1NT	4♠

West leads the ♡J. Obviously the ♡A is wrong and that suggests that the ◊A won't be right either. What is your best chance of avoiding four losers?

You will find a clue in the last hand, in the last two for that matter. Give East a chance to err. He doesn't know your shape. You could have a singleton heart and ◊Kxx, and if so, it would be vital for him to win the first trick so as to play a diamond through the closed hand. Otherwise you would have time to set up a heart trick for a diamond discard. Pretend that that's how it is. Play low from dummy. It will cost nothing. If East doesn't rise with the ♡A you will be able to discard a club loser on a heart honour later. If he goes up with the ace, you are home. This was the deal in full, and just for the record, East rose with the ♡A and the story had a happy ending — for South.

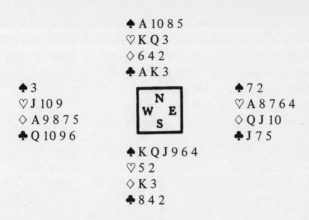

♠ A 10 8 5
♥ K Q 3
♦ 6 4 2
♣ A K 3

♠ 3
♥ J 10 9
♦ A 9 8 7 5
♣ Q 10 9 6

♠ 7 2
♥ A 8 7 6 4
♦ Q J 10
♣ J 7 5

♠ K Q J 9 6 4
♥ 5 2
♦ K 3
♣ 8 4 2

Don't blame East. No one can guess right all the time.

FACES ALTER CASES

The technician draws all his inferences from the bidding and the play. The psychologist gives pride of place to the players. The same bid, in the same situation, means one thing when the bidder is A and another when it's B.

The play of an ace by Henri Svarc carries one message. The same play by a less distinguished defender would carry another — or maybe none at all.

I know of no better illustration of 'playing the players' than this hand from rubber bridge in the days when the great Adam Meredith was in his prime. 'Plum', as he was always known, bid spades in and out of season, not because he had them, but to prevent the other side from bidding them. He took risks against the strongest opponents. He took may more against weaker ones.

Sitting South in a London club, with Meredith on his left, Michael Wolach picked up:

♠7 ♥QJ98 ♦Q1083 ♣KQ109

Dealer, at favourable vulnerability, Meredith opened 1♠. Wolach's partner, an excitable young man with no hope of ever reaching second-class status, bid 4♠, promptly doubled by Meredith's partner. Fearing the worst, most players in Wolach's place would grind their teeth or put on a sickly smile. Wolach redoubled!

He reasoned that his mediocre partner, who rightly stood in awe of

Meredith, wouldn't have dared to soar into 4♠ unless he had plenty in reserve. No one took liberties against Plum. Ready to punish severely any attempt by opponents to escape, Wolach knew it was safe to redouble. His psychology brought its reward when a jittery but jubilant partner brought home twelve tricks on:

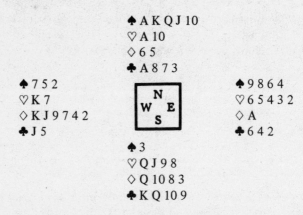

```
                    ♠ A K Q J 10
                    ♡ A 10
                    ◇ 6 5
                    ♣ A 8 7 3
  ♠ 7 5 2                              ♠ 9 8 6 4
  ♡ K 7              N                 ♡ 6 5 4 3 2
  ◇ K J 9 7 4 2   W     E              ◇ A
  ♣ J 5              S                 ♣ 6 4 2
                    ♠ 3
                    ♡ Q J 9 8
                    ◇ Q 10 8 3
                    ♣ K Q 10 9
```

At times, technique, talent, psychology and imagination all combine in equal measure to shape a bidding sequence or a line of play. At others, this or that factor predominates, and on occasion suffices by itself, independently of the others. On the last six hands psychology had pride of place. Let us now turn the spotlight on imagination. The two are often integral parts of the same process, but it needn't be so. To isolate imagination we'll start with a clear-cut example in which psychology plays no part.

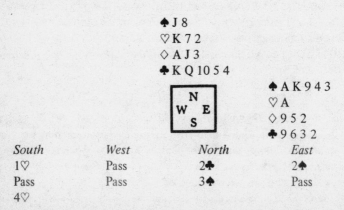

```
                    ♠ J 8
                    ♡ K 7 2
                    ◇ A J 3
                    ♣ K Q 10 5 4
                                      ♠ A K 9 4 3
                      N               ♡ A
                   W     E            ◇ 9 5 2
                      S               ♣ 9 6 3 2
```

South	West	North	East
1♡	Pass	2♣	2♠
Pass	Pass	3♠	Pass
4♡			

West leads the ♠6 to East's king and ace, following with the ♠2 on the second round. Declarer's cards are ♠7 and ♠10.

There's scarcely anything left on the bidding for West, at best the ◇K or the ♡Q. If it's the ◇K it's useless. The finesse will succeed, and yet . . .

At trick three East played a third spade. In with the ♠Q, declarer led the ♡J and ran it. Winning with the ♡A, East played a fourth spade.

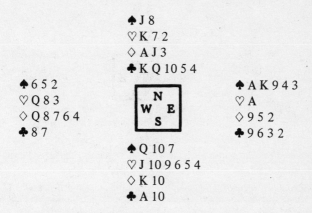

```
              ♠ J 8
              ♡ K 7 2
              ◇ A J 3
              ♣ K Q 10 5 4
♠ 6 5 2                        ♠ A K 9 4 3
♡ Q 8 3          N            ♡ A
◇ Q 8 7 6 4   W     E         ◇ 9 5 2
♣ 8 7            S            ♣ 9 6 3 2
              ♠ Q 10 7
              ♡ J 10 9 6 5 4
              ◇ K 10
              ♣ A 10
```

If South ruffs with the ♡10(9) West discards and remains with the ♡Q8, a certain trick. If South doesn't ruff, the ♡8 will drive out the king with the same result.

Placing West with the ♡Q wasn't difficult, but only an imaginative defender would have visualised the ♡8, the key card to ensure promotion for the badly placed queen.

Declarer cannot be seriously faulted for playing the ♡J. He had to find the queen and he couldn't guess that the ♡A was bare.

It may not look like it, but the next hand is very similar to the one above.

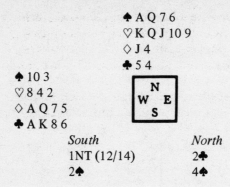

♠ A Q 7 6
♡ K Q J 10 9
◇ J 4
♣ 5 4

♠ 10 3
♡ 8 4 2
◇ A Q 7 5
♣ A K 8 6

South	North
1NT (12/14)	2♣
2♠	4♠

You lead the ♣K, the ♣7 from partner, the ♣9 from declarer. What are your thought processes as you look for a way to defeat the contract?

You have two tricks in clubs, and with no hope of another in hearts, you will need two diamonds. But you must seize them quickly for once declarer gains the lead he will score ten tricks with: four spades, five hearts and a diamond ruff in the closed hand, after discarding two diamonds on dummy's hearts — three if his pattern is 4-2-4-3.

Can partner have the ◇K? Impossible. Allowing South 12 points for the barest no trump and adding them to the 26 you can see in your hand and in dummy, all that remains for East is 0-2. If it's zero there can be no defence, so the only tangible hope is that partner's maximum holding, a queen, is the ♣Q.

Again, your imagination is focused on a particular card, and visualising it in partner's hand, you underlead your ♣A at trick two, put him in and snatch two tricks in diamonds while there's still time.

Partner may not have the ♣Q, of course, but except in a pairs event, you have nothing to lose and everything to gain by assuming that he has.

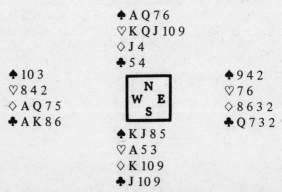

♠ A Q 7 6
♡ K Q J 10 9
◇ J 4
♣ 5 4

♠ 10 3
♡ 8 4 2
◇ A Q 7 5
♣ A K 8 6

♠ 9 4 2
♡ 7 6
◇ 8 6 3 2
♣ Q 7 3 2

♠ K J 8 5
♡ A 5 3
◇ K 10 9
♣ J 10 9

Imagination usually calls for something more, at times much more, than visualising a single card. Let us now watch Rafael Munoz, the Velasquez of Spanish bridge.

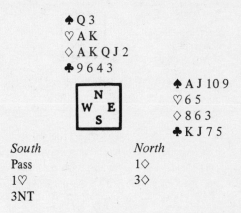

♠ Q 3
♡ A K
♢ A K Q J 2
♣ 9 6 4 3

♠ A J 10 9
♡ 6 5
♢ 8 6 3
♣ K J 7 5

South	North
Pass	1♢
1♡	3♢
3NT	

West leads the ♡J. At trick two declarer plays dummy's ♠3. Sitting East, Munoz could see seven solid tricks in dummy and the ♡Q, by inference, in the closed hand. The ♠K — declarer obviously had it — would be his ninth trick. There was, therefore, not a moment to lose. To beat the contract the defence would somehow have to score four tricks in clubs. Partner could be credited with the ♣A, for otherwise there was no hope, but it was too much to place him with the ♣Q, too. Assuming, then, that South had the ♣Q, how could the suit be played to yield the defence four tricks?

Munoz drew on his vivid imagination to conjure up the only distribution to serve his purpose, and the gods rewarded him, for this was the deal:

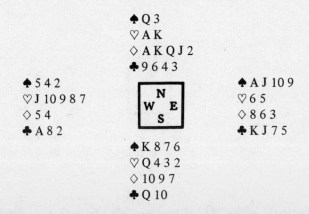

♠ Q 3
♡ A K
♢ A K Q J 2
♣ 9 6 4 3

♠ 5 4 2
♡ J 10 9 8 7
♢ 5 4
♣ A 8 2

♠ A J 10 9
♡ 6 5
♢ 8 6 3
♣ K J 7 5

♠ K 8 7 6
♡ Q 4 3 2
♢ 10 9 7
♣ Q 10

Going up at trick two with the ♠A, Rafael Munoz laid down the ♣K, West playing the ♣8, not as a come-on signal, but to unblock. The ♣5 to the ace picked up South's queen and the ♣2 now pierced dummy's ♣96. The ♣10 and the ♣8 could have changed places without affecting the issue — so long as West unblocked.

IMAGINATION CHANGES SIDES

There is most scope for imagination in defence, but it can be the key to success in every part of the game, as here:

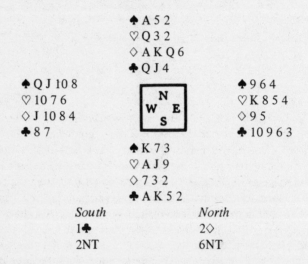

```
              ♠ A 5 2
              ♡ Q 3 2
              ◇ A K Q 6
              ♣ Q J 4
♠ Q J 10 8                    ♠ 9 6 4
♡ 10 7 6          N           ♡ K 8 5 4
◇ J 10 8 4     W     E        ◇ 9 5
♣ 8 7             S           ♣ 10 9 6 3
              ♠ K 7 3
              ♡ A J 9
              ◇ 7 3 2
              ♣ A K 5 2
```

South	North
1♣	2◇
2NT	6NT

West leads the ♠Q.

Declarer has ten top tricks and can quickly develop an eleventh in hearts. The twelfth would appear to depend on a 3–3 diamond break or on a rather unlikely squeeze in spades and diamonds, the defender who is long in diamonds having five or more spades.

The first move is to test the hearts. At trick two declarer leads dummy's ♡2 and inserts the ♡J. It holds. Now there are real chances of a squeeze in the red suits. To rectify the count South plays low spades from both hands. West wins and returns another spade.

The stage has been set. Four cards have gone, three spades and a heart. After four clubs neither defender in the 5-card ending will be able to keep two hearts and four diamonds. There's just one snag. What can declarer throw from dummy on his fourth club? A heart,

baring the queen? Then East, if he has the long diamond, can throw a
heart, too — unless he has the ♡10 as well as the ♡K.

South foresees this situation — that is a matter of technique — and
calls on his imagination to conjure up a picture in which either defender
could be squeezed no matter which one has the ♡10. In with the ♠K
at trick four, he crosses in clubs and leads the ♡Q, forcing East to
cover. Now he plays out his clubs, coming down to:

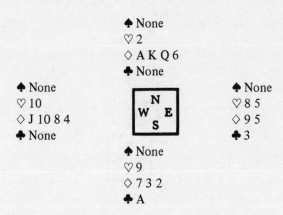

On the ♣A West is squeezed. If East had the ♡10 and long diamonds,
he, too, would be squeezed. His hand could be:

♠ 964 ♡ K105 ◇ J1095 ♣ 1096

Here, as in our first two examples, declarer's imagination was again
focused on one particular card, the ♡10. The rest was technique, but
by itself it would not have sufficed.

COMBINATION PUNCH

What if no distribution can yield declarer the tricks he needs? Then, combining psychology with imagination, the resourceful player conjures up in the minds of defenders a scenario in which they do for declarer what he cannot do for himself.

Here is Gabriel Chagas playing against Israel in the 1980 Olympiad.

```
              ♠ 6
              ♡ K J 7
              ◇ 4 2
              ♣ A 10 8 7 5 4 2

♠ A 10 7 4          N          ♠ Q 9 5 2
♡ A 8 4        W       E       ♡ 5 3
◇ Q 10 8            S          ◇ J 9 6 5 3
♣ K 9 3                        ♣ Q 6

              ♠ K J 8 3
              ♡ Q 10 9 6 2
              ◇ A K 7
              ♣ J
```

West leads the ♡4 against 4♡, killing one of dummy's entries from the start. Where can declarer find ten tricks? The one thing in his favour is that East doesn't know that West has the ♡A. Making the most of it, Chagas set out to persuade East that he intended to establish the clubs.

Winning the first trick with dummy's ♡7, he came to hand with a diamond and ran the ♣J. East won and, to attack dummy's illusory trump entries to the clubs, promptly switched to the ♠Q. Chagas ducked smoothly. A second spade to the king and ace was ruffed in dummy and now Gabriel Chagas had ten tricks — four hearts, a spade, two spade ruffs in dummy, the ◇AK and the ♣A.

The Israelis, who could have so easily broken the contract, were left to console themselves with the reflection that to be taken in by so artistic an illusionist as Chagas was no disgrace.

France's Pierre Jaïs and Roger Trézel will always rank as one of the leading pairs in the annals of bridge. This is a hand from the Bermuda Bowl finals in 1971, which impressed Jaïs.

Bobby Wolff, sitting South, holds:

♠ A102 ♡ AKQJ1052 ◇ KQ4 ♣ None

South	*West*	*North*	*East*
Wolff	Trézel	Jacoby	Jaïs
1♣	3♣	Dble	5♣
?			

The 1♣ opening shows a minimum of 17 points. Jacoby's double promises not less than 6, but without three controls, a king ranking as one control, an ace as two.

What should Bobby Wolff do over the barrage bid of 5♣?

Bobby reasoned that Jacoby's 6 points must be precisely where he wanted them and so, without running any risks, he bid 6♡. Jacoby duly put down:

♠ KQ63 ♡ 863 ♢ J76 ♣ J64

The unbeatable slam was missed by the French in the other room.

Jaïs told me when we discussed the Taipeh finals in Paris: "I had never met Corn's Dallas Aces before, but I knew that they trained intensively, with a computer and everything that a bridge laboratory could provide. So I expected a team of soulless scientists, ruthlessly efficient, but lacking in the finer points of human understanding." The psychology and imagination of the Aces deeply impressed him.

It's your turn to be West, holding:

♠ A963 ♡ 52 ♢ J853 ♣ QJ9

At Love All, with your side silent, the bidding has proceeded.

South	*North*
—	1NT (12/14)
3♡	4♣
4♢	5♢
5♡	6♡

What do you lead? Without any strain on your imagination you can tell that North has a good fit for hearts, the ♣A and the ♢K, and since he made a further effort over 4♢, he doubtless has a maximum no trump. Knowing all that, South was, however, prepared to settle for 5♡. Why? Clearly because he feared losing two spades. Well aware of South's fears, North nevertheless bid 6♡. It follows that he must have the second round control in spades. It can't be a singleton, since he opened 1NT, and if it's ♠KQ there's no hope, but it could be KJx or simply Kxx.

Having applied psychology to your analysis of the bidding, it's time to switch on the imagination. Given time, declarer might be able to discard one of his spade losers, or both, on something in dummy. Alternatively, the ♠A being under the king, he cannot go wrong, unless the ♠J is in dummy, too, and then he may still make the right guess.

So spades must be attacked at once. Lead a low one. Since leading from an ace against a slam is unusual, if any guess is involved, declarer is likely to misguess.

This was the deal when the hand came up at rubber bridge.

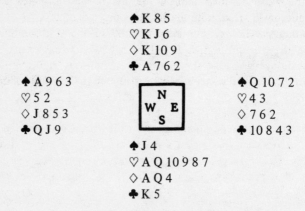

```
              ♠ K 8 5
              ♡ K J 6
              ◇ K 10 9
              ♣ A 7 6 2
♠ A 9 6 3                    ♠ Q 10 7 2
♡ 5 2          N            ♡ 4 3
◇ J 8 5 3    W   E          ◇ 7 6 2
♣ Q J 9        S            ♣ 10 8 4 3
              ♠ J 4
              ♡ A Q 10 9 8 7
              ◇ A Q 4
              ♣ K 5
```

No one, not even partner, could blame declarer for playing low from dummy and going down like a gentleman.

Observe that, left to his own devices, declarer cannot go wrong. With no way of parking a spade he must play West for the ace. He has no choice but to make his contract — unless you provide him with a losing option.

Can you make certain of your modest contract of 3NT on these good-looking hands with 28 combined points and a respectable 6-card suit in dummy?

```
  ♠ K Q 3                    ♠ A 4 2
  ♡ A K 3 2       N         ♡ 8 6
  ◇ A K 5 3     W   E       ◇ 9 7
  ♣ Q 3           S         ♣ K 10 9 8 6 4
      West                    East
      2NT                     3NT
```

North leads the ♠J. It's not a bad slam to be in, but you are only in game, so how do you play? If, winning in hand, you lead the ♣Q, it will hold. A second club may be won by South, and if he started with ♣AJ2, the club suit will be dead and the contract with it, for in no way can you develop a ninth trick.

Bad luck! In a slam it would be fatal, but in a mere game there's a way of circumventing it.

At trick two lead the ♣3 and insert dummy's ♣10. Should South take the trick with the ♣J, you will win his return in hand and over-take the ♣Q in dummy, clearing the suit. If the ♣10 holds, a club to your queen will set up your ninth trick, come what may.

Neither psychology nor imagination, nor the two combined, will suffice to find this simple ingenious solution. It calls for a 'sudden happy thought', one of the dictionary definitions of *inspiration*, and that brings us to the steps leading to the next, brilliantly illuminated chamber.

CHAPTER THREE

The Sixth and other Senses

We have reached the top of the golden cupola over the temple, with its spire pointing straight at Olympus. Combined with technique, psychology, imagination, but transcending them all, another attribute here comes into play – inspiration. Easy to recognise, yet hard to define, in poetry it would be called the 'divine spark'. In bridge we have nothing better than 'brilliance', a term which hardly describes a feat such as this:

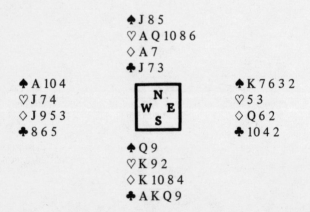

```
                    ♠ J 8 5
                    ♡ A Q 10 8 6
                    ◇ A 7
                    ♣ J 7 3
  ♠ A 10 4                        ♠ K 7 6 3 2
  ♡ J 7 4          N              ♡ 5 3
  ◇ J 9 5 3     W     E           ◇ Q 6 2
  ♣ 8 6 5          S              ♣ 10 4 2
                    ♠ Q 9
                    ♡ K 9 2
                    ◇ K 10 8 4
                    ♣ A K Q 9
```

After an uncontested auction in a pairs event in France, North–South reached the undignified contract of 6NT with two top losers. In mitigation of the offence, they could plead that being up against one of the strongest pairs in the country, and feeling outclassed, they were justified in gambling.

West led the ◇3 to East's ◇Q. How do you suppose that South found a way of making twelve tricks? Look for the divine spark, for nothing else will do.

With nerves of steel, South allowed the ◇Q to hold! Of course, if

East had the ♠A he would go down at once — instead of later. But half the time West would have it and then, if his luck held, he might stand a chance.

East returned another diamond to dummy's ace and now declarer proceeded to reel off nine more winners, discarding the ♠Q9 on dummy's hearts. Which two cards should West retain at the end? Clinging on to his ♠A — and who wouldn't? — he let go his fourth diamond, and now the ◇8 brought declarer his twelfth trick.

West took the blame. At trick two East had returned the ◇6. With four diamonds he would have played the lowest, so West should have counted the suit better. Maybe, but it's hard to defend against an inspired declarer.

The gods, and more especially the goddesses, are kind to the bold, and Venus, or it may have been Pallas Athena, threw up a cloud of dust to help her favourite. He deserved every speck of it.

Still in France, we find this spectacular coup described in *Le Bridgeur*.

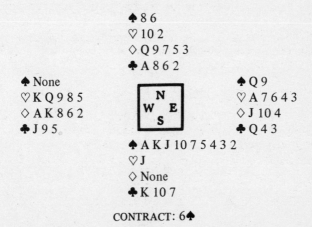

♠ 8 6
♡ 10 2
◇ Q 9 7 5 3
♣ A 8 6 2

♠ None
♡ K Q 9 8 5
◇ A K 8 6 2
♣ J 9 5

♠ Q 9
♡ A 7 6 4 3
◇ J 10 4
♣ Q 4 3

♠ A K J 10 7 5 4 3 2
♡ J
◇ None
♣ K 10 7

CONTRACT: 6♠

West, who had called 2♡ over South's opening 2♣, led the ◇K. How did South contrive to make twelve tricks? This time there's not a particle of dust in the cloudless sky. Even looking at all four hands the answer isn't apparent. Declarer, still in his early twenties, found it in a flash. On the ◇K he threw the ♡J!

West switched to the ♡K, but it was already too late. The count had been rectified for a deadly double squeeze from which there could be no escape. The heart ruff at trick two was followed by eight spades. When the last one settled on the table, this was the 4-card ending:

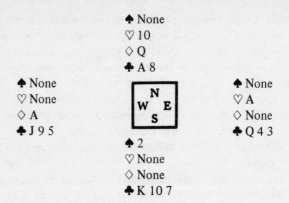

```
                    ♠ None
                    ♡ 10
                    ◇ Q
                    ♣ A 8
♠ None                                    ♠ None
♡ None          ┌─────────┐               ♡ A
◇ A             │    N    │               ◇ None
♣ J 9 5         │  W   E  │               ♣ Q 4 3
                │    S    │
                └─────────┘
                    ♠ 2
                    ♡ None
                    ◇ None
                    ♣ K 10 7
```

To retain the ◇A West was forced to shed a club. Having served her purpose, the ◇Q was thrown from dummy and it was East's turn to squirm. He had to keep the ♡A, the ♡10 being still in dummy, so he too parted with a club and South's third club became a winner.

Had West kept the ♡Q in the 3-card ending, allowing East to retain three clubs, he would have had to bare the ♣J, and with a perfect count on his hand, declarer would have executed a *guard squeeze*, dropping West's ♣J and taking the marked finesse against East's ♣Q.

"I DON'T BELIEVE IT"

A truly inspired defence against Italy's Frederico Mayer in an international pairs event earned France's Gilles Cohen the much-coveted Bols brilliancy prize. But was it just brilliance?

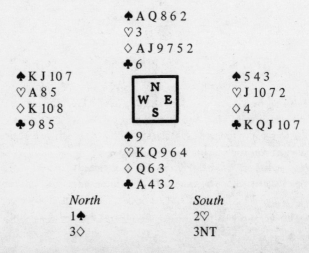

```
                    ♠ A Q 8 6 2
                    ♡ 3
                    ◇ A J 9 7 5 2
                    ♣ 6
♠ K J 10 7                                ♠ 5 4 3
♡ A 8 5         ┌─────────┐               ♡ J 10 7 2
◇ K 10 8        │    N    │               ◇ 4
♣ 9 8 5         │  W   E  │               ♣ K Q J 10 7
                │    S    │
                └─────────┘
                    ♠ 9
                    ♡ K Q 9 6 4
                    ◇ Q 6 3
                    ♣ A 4 3 2
```

	North		*South*
	1♠		2♡
	3◇		3NT

Sitting West, Cohen led the ♠J, taken in dummy with the ♠Q. To keep communications open, Mayer began with the ◇2 to his queen. A club switch, driving out the only entry to his hand, would have embarrassed declarer, but Cohen couldn't see the other hands, so he found another way. Can you guess what it was?

He allowed the ◇Q to hold!

When Cohen followed to the second diamond Mayer was in no doubt that East, with ◇Kx, had made a daring play on the first round. That West should give up a certain trick for no apparent reason was surely impossible.

By finessing, Mayer could have made certain of his contract — and playing for money or IMPs he would have doubtless done so — but in a pairs event the extra trick makes a big difference. So he went up confidently with the ◇A, and now the diamonds, instead of being worth five tricks, brought in just two.

Gilles Cohen's was a risky play, but its sheer audacity ensured its safety. When, instead of dropping the ◇K, East showed out on the ace, Mayer must have felt like the old lady who exclaimed, when she first saw a giraffe, "I don't believe it."

AN IMPERATIVE DISCARD

The scene is a key match in the tournament for the Vanderbilt Cup, one of the principal trophies in American bridge.

Both vul: dealer South

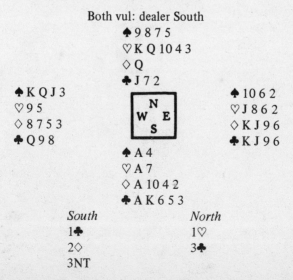

♠ 9 8 7 5
♡ K Q 10 4 3
◇ Q
♣ J 7 2

♠ K Q J 3   ♠ 10 6 2
♡ 9 5   ♡ J 8 6 2
◇ 8 7 5 3   ◇ K J 9 6
♣ Q 9 8   ♣ K J 9 6

♠ A 4
♡ A 7
◇ A 10 4 2
♣ A K 6 5 3

South	North
1♣	1♡
2◇	3♣
3NT	

West leads the ♠K. Declarer wins and tests the hearts. When, on the third round, West shows out, he turns to the clubs. The ♣Q doesn't drop, however, and West is in.

Looking at all four hands, it is apparent that only by leading the ♠3 can West break the contract. Anything else and declarer will quickly wrap up nine tricks. Since West can't see the other hands, and more especially the ♠10, it's up to East to inform him. How can he do it?

East must find a discard on the ♣Q, but no signal yet invented will show the ♠10. This is the time for inspiration, and when this hand came up, East found it. On the ♣Q he threw the ◊K! The message was unmistakable. Diamonds offered no hope, so something else did. Otherwise East wouldn't wantonly throw away a potential trick. West duly returned the ♠3, allowing East to score the ♡J before returning his third spade.

THE DUELLISTS

Sitting East-West are Omar Sharif and Benito Garozzo. Facing them are Paul Hackett and Martin Hoffman.

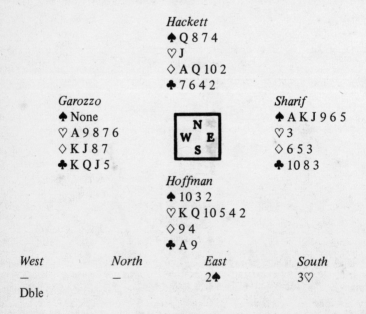

Hackett
♠ Q 8 7 4
♡ J
◊ A Q 10 2
♣ 7 6 4 2

Garozzo
♠ None
♡ A 9 8 7 6
◊ K J 8 7
♣ K Q J 5

Sharif
♠ A K J 9 6 5
♡ 3
◊ 6 5 3
♣ 10 8 3

Hoffman
♠ 10 3 2
♡ K Q 10 5 4 2
◊ 9 4
♣ A 9

West	North	East	South
—	—	2♠	3♡
Dble			

Omar Sharif's 2♠ was the weak variety, showing a 6-card suit and 8-10 points.

Benito led the ♡6 to dummy's ♡J. At trick two, Martin Hoffman played a club, inserting the ♣9.

What is your forecast? Will Hoffman make his contract or will Garozzo get the better of him?

Hoffman's plan was to cash the ♣A, take a double finesse in diamonds and ruff two clubs in the closed hand. The ◇A would be cashed before the second ruff, bringing him a total of seven tricks — ♡J, ♣A, two club ruffs, and three diamonds. With the ♡KQ10 intact he would be certain of two more tricks.

Alas, the best-laid schemes of mice and experts aft gang aglee. Coming in with the ♣J at trick two, Garozzo returned — the ◇K!

This pinned the lead in dummy and killed a vital entry before declarer was ready to use it.

No player visits the golden cupola more frequently than Benito Garozzo.

SPOT THE ENTRY

We are back in France with no big names this time among the dramatis personae.

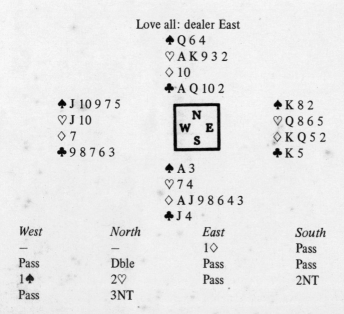

```
                    Love all: dealer East
                    ♠ Q 6 4
                    ♡ A K 9 3 2
                    ◇ 10
                    ♣ A Q 10 2
  ♠ J 10 9 7 5            N            ♠ K 8 2
  ♡ J 10            W         E        ♡ Q 8 6 5
  ◇ 7                    S            ◇ K Q 5 2
  ♣ 9 8 7 6 3                          ♣ K 5
                    ♠ A 3
                    ♡ 7 4
                    ◇ A J 9 8 6 4 3
                    ♣ J 4
```

West	North	East	South
—	—	1◇	Pass
Pass	Dble	Pass	Pass
1♠	2♡	Pass	2NT
Pass	3NT		

West led the ♠J, the ♠4 from dummy, the ♠8 from East. Winning with
the ♠A, declarer crossed in hearts and played the ◊10, covered by East
and won in hand. The ◊J was allowed to hold. A third diamond was
taken by East, who returned a heart, locking declarer in dummy.

Having scored five tricks — the ♠A, ◊A, ◊J and ♡AK — South
needed four more. But at this point he had already made certain of
them. The key play came earlier. On the ◊J (trick four) he threw
dummy's ♣A! On the next diamond he jettisoned the ♣Q. And now a
club provided an escape from dummy. East could take three more
tricks — the ♠K and the ♡Q8 — but whatever he did next, the ♣J
ensured an entry to the diamonds.

East shouldn't have covered the ◊10, clearly an error, but then
taking advantage of opponents' lapses is one of the most rewarding
skills at bridge. Sometimes it calls for inspiration.

LA BELLE HÉLÈNE

No one had more flashes of inspiration than Charles Goren's favourite
partner, Helen Sobel, one of the very few women who could hold her
own among the best players of the day, a day that saw Howard Schenken
and Johnny Crawford in their prime.

Helen was South here in the 1958 Vanderbilt.

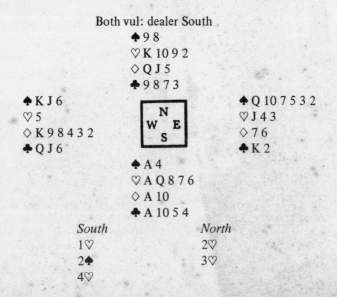

Both vul: dealer South
```
                    ♠ 9 8
                    ♡ K 10 9 2
                    ◊ Q J 5
                    ♣ 9 8 7 3
  ♠ K J 6                          ♠ Q 10 7 5 3 2
  ♡ 5               N              ♡ J 4 3
  ◊ K 9 8 4 3 2   W   E            ◊ 7 6
  ♣ Q J 6           S              ♣ K 2
                    ♠ A 4
                    ♡ A Q 8 7 6
                    ◊ A 10
                    ♣ A 10 5 4
```

South	*North*
1♡	2♡
2♠	3♡
4♡	

Helen Sobel's 2♠, though ostensibly a trial bid, was designed mainly to stop a spade lead. With no interest in spades, West led the ♣Q, won by the ace. The ♡A and ♡Q followed, West signalling with the ◇9.

Deciding correctly that the diamond finesse was doomed, how should declarer proceed? East's doubleton diamond is not on view, but the possibility was not to be overlooked.

It is tempting to draw East's last trump and continue with the ◇A and ◇10, setting up a trick to take care of the losing spade. It won't work, because West will surely knock out the ♠A and dummy's fourth trump will be the only entry to the established diamond. Declarer will have to give up the lead twice in clubs and will have one trump only left to stem the flow of hostile spades and diamonds.

Would it be better to take two rounds of diamonds without drawing East's trump? That wouldn't be any good either because West would promptly lead a third diamond for East to ruff, and even if South could over-ruff, the spade loser would remain.

This is the time to blend talent with technique. Any ideas?

Helen Sobel's solution was to lead the ◇10 away from the ace! Winning the spade return, she cashed the ◇A, crossed in trumps, removing East's knave, and discarded her spade loser in all safety on the ◇Q. That left her with two trumps, a move ahead of the opposition.

Simple. Talented play so often is.

My next example is taken from Pietro Forquet's column in beautifully produced *Bridge d'Italia*, always brimming with interesting material.

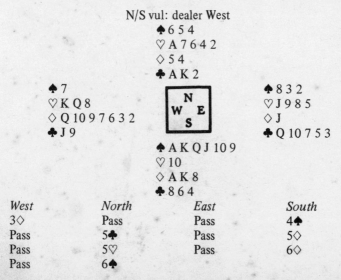

N/S vul: dealer West

```
              ♠ 6 5 4
              ♡ A 7 6 4 2
              ◇ 5 4
              ♣ A K 2
♠ 7                              ♠ 8 3 2
♡ K Q 8          N              ♡ J 9 8 5
◇ Q 10 9 7 6 3 2  W   E          ◇ J
♣ J 9                S          ♣ Q 10 7 5 3
              ♠ A K Q J 10 9
              ♡ 10
              ◇ A K 8
              ♣ 8 6 4
```

West	North	East	South
3◇	Pass	Pass	4♠
Pass	5♣	Pass	5◇
Pass	5♡	Pass	6◇
Pass	6♠		

West leads the ♡K. How should South play? If trumps are 2–2 and hearts 4–3 declarer has thirteen tricks. Two rounds of trumps dispel that illusion. The squeeze specialist will hope to find East vulnerable to a squeeze in hearts and clubs. This would call for a very unlikely scenario.

Pietro Forquet points to a far better, simpler way to tackle the problem.

After the ♡A and two rounds of trumps, South cashes the ◊A and, crossing to the ♣A, leads a diamond. If East ruffs it's all over. Dummy's third club is parked on the ◊K and the club loser disappears. Too wily a bird to fall into the trap, East throws a club. South wins, but he still has two losers, a club and a diamond. An elegant variation on the loser-on-loser theme causes one of them to vanish. Having scored the ◊K, South leads the ◊8 and throws on it dummy's ♣2. Whatever West does next, declarer cashes the ♣K – the ♣A has gone – comes to hand with a heart and ruffs the last club.

There can be no better illustration of the divine spark which poets so rightly praise, than this hand, played by Forquet's *squadra azzurra* team mate, Giorgio Belladonna. The scene was Winnipeg in 1971 during Omar Sharif's series of matches against Ira Corn's Aces.

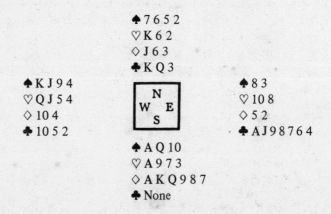

```
                    ♠ 7 6 5 2
                    ♡ K 6 2
                    ◊ J 6 3
                    ♣ K Q 3
♠ K J 9 4                              ♠ 8 3
♡ Q J 5 4          N                   ♡ 10 8
◊ 10 4          W     E                ◊ 5 2
♣ 10 5 2           S                   ♣ A J 9 8 7 6 4
                    ♠ A Q 10
                    ♡ A 9 7 3
                    ◊ A K Q 9 8 7
                    ♣ None
```

Both Easts, first to speak at favourable vulnerability, opened 4♣ and both Souths became declarers in 6◊. Again, in both rooms the lead was a club to the queen and ace, ruffed in the closed hand.

Even with all cards on view, it's hard to see how, with everything wrong, the contract can be made. It looks as if the spade finesse cannot be avoided. The American declarer took it and went one down. Giorgio reasoned that with the ♠K East would have had too much to pre-empt, so this is how he played.

After three rounds of trumps, ending in dummy, he threw the ♠10 on the ♣Q and ruffed a club, bringing about this position:

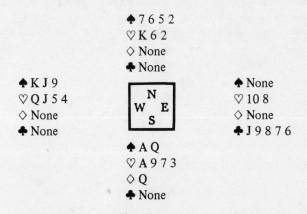

```
              ♠ 7 6 5 2
              ♡ K 6 2
              ◊ None
              ♣ None
♠ K J 9        ┌───────┐      ♠ None
♡ Q J 5 4      │   N   │      ♡ 10 8
◊ None         │ W   E │      ◊ None
♣ None         │   S   │      ♣ J 9 8 7 6
              └───────┘
              ♠ A Q
              ♡ A 9 7 3
              ◊ Q
              ♣ None
```

The ◊Q, Belladonna's last trump, turned the heat on West. If he threw a heart, three rounds of hearts would put him on play, compelling a lead into the ♠AQ. If he shed a spade, the ♠A, followed by the ♠Q, would set up two spades in dummy.

THE COUP THAT NEVER WAS

A great hand, yet it must yield precedence to the next one, which is
surely the greatest of Giorgio Belladonna's dummy plays.

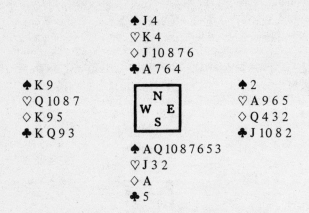

```
                      ♠ J 4
                      ♡ K 4
                      ◇ J 10 8 7 6
                      ♣ A 7 6 4
      ♠ K 9                              ♠ 2
      ♡ Q 10 8 7          N             ♡ A 9 6 5
      ◇ K 9 5         W       E         ◇ Q 4 3 2
      ♣ K Q 9 3           S             ♣ J 10 8 2
                      ♠ A Q 10 8 7 6 5 3
                      ♡ J 3 2
                      ◇ A
                      ♣ 5
```

West leads a diamond against 4♠. How can declarer make certain of
the contract against any possible distribution?

Even given time, the answer isn't easy to find. Belladonna, I was told,
found it in a flash, without so much as batting the proverbial eyelid.

Crossing to dummy at trick two, with a club to the ace, he led the
♡4 away from the king. It's the perfect safety play. It wouldn't matter,
of course, if East had the ♡Q as well as the ♡A. So long as the ♣A
isn't ruffed declarer cannot lose more than two hearts and a trump.

Where was the hand played? In a European Championship according
to one version. In a tournament in Venice, according to another.

When I asked Giorgio himself he swore that he had never seen the
hand before and knew nothing whatever about it. All the writers who
had ascribed it to him, and I was one of them, had been the victims
of a delusion.

A masterpiece had come to light. No one seemed to know the origin,
so by common consent it was ascribed to Giorgio Belladonna.

Se non e vero e ben trovato

Could there be a greater tribute to a player's genius?

VIBRATIONS

Just as the accomplished player is quick to punish technical errors, so he knows how to pick up the vibrations round the table, the unconscious mannerisms which betray confidence and unease, the barely perceptible pauses reflecting the doubts, the hopes and fears behind the impassive faces of the players.

No one had finer antennae than Maurice Harrison-Gray, a giant during the *grande époque* of British bridge. This was one of his spectacular coups.

At a decisive moment in a match against a top-class team, Gray sat East.

Love all: dealer East

	♠ A K Q			♠ 10 5 3
	♡ A 9 3	**N**		♡ K Q 8 7 6
	◇ K Q J 2	**W E**		◇ A
	♣ Q 7 4	**S**		♣ A J 10 6

West	East
—	1♡
3◇	4♣
4♠	5◇
7♡	

South led a spade.

Opponents had taken no part in the bidding, but over 7♡ North had paused before passing. He must have had something to think about. Gray wondered what it was. Only a freakish hand and the thought of a sacrifice could explain the pause. At equal vulnerability it was most unlikely that he would consider paying the price with two heart losers, so he was surely marked with a void or a singleton. If South had all five trumps there was nothing to be done, but if the division was 4–1 there was a chance and Harrison Gray proceeded to take it.

The correct play in trumps was, of course, to start with the ace. Then, if South showed out, North's J10, though thrice guarded, could be picked up. But since it was South, not North, who had the length in trumps, the 'correct' play wouldn't do. Gray began by leading the ♡3 away from the ace. When North produced the ♡10, he gave an inward cry of triumph and going up with the ♡K proceeded to finesse the ♡9. It held! North's hand was:

♠ J987542   ♡ 10   ◇ 9   ♣ K985

Gray couldn't help wondering what his team-mates would have said had North produced the ♡J.

SPLIT-SECOND TIMING

In politics, according to Lord Wilson, a week is a long time. In bridge it can be a split second.

Declarer here is Renée Zwaan, playing for Holland against Panama in the 1980 Olumpiad.

    ♠ Q J
    ♡ A Q 9 7
    ◇ K 7 5 3
    ♣ A 6 3

    ♠ A 10 9 8 4 3
    ♡ J
    ◇ A Q 9 8
    ♣ J 7

After six rounds of bidding, during which East doubled North's cue-bid of 5♡, Renée Zwaan found herself in 6♠.

West led the ♡4 to dummy's ♡A. The contract appears to depend on the trump finesse, and at trick two declarer duly led the ♠Q which held. There was, however, a barely perceptible pause before West followed with the ♠2. How should the play proceed?

Renée Zwaan changed her plan at once. Abandoning the trump finesse, she ruffed a heart, noting West's ♡6, and continued with the ♠A and ♠10. As she suspected, West had the king.

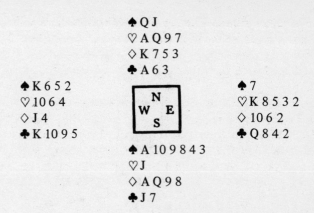

```
              ♠ Q J
              ♡ A Q 9 7
              ◇ K 7 5 3
              ♣ A 6 3
♠ K 6 5 2                      ♠ 7
♡ 10 6 4        N             ♡ K 8 5 3 2
◇ J 4        W     E          ◇ 10 6 2
♣ K 10 9 5      S             ♣ Q 8 4 2
              ♠ A 10 9 8 4 3
              ♡ J
              ◇ A Q 9 8
              ♣ J 7
```

Winning the club return with the ♣A, she led the ♡Q, forcing the king from East and scooping the ten. Back with the ◇A, Renée drew the last trump and claimed.

A split-second's hesitation, overlooked by the other five senses, allowed the sixth to alert her and bring home a contract which destiny had surely intended to fail.

MISSING A BEAT

For the other side of the medal we turn to another Olympiad, sixteen years earlier, at Miami.

It was tough pounding between the Americans and the *squadra azzurra*, never more than a few IMPs apart, when this hand came up.

Love all: dealer North

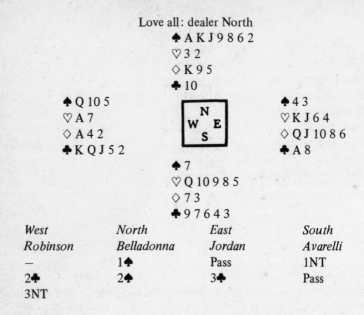

♠ A K J 9 8 6 2
♡ 3 2
◇ K 9 5
♣ 10

♠ Q 10 5
♡ A 7
◇ A 4 2
♣ K Q J 5 2

♠ 4 3
♡ K J 6 4
◇ Q J 10 8 6
♣ A 8

♠ 7
♡ Q 10 9 8 5
◇ 7 3
♣ 9 7 6 4 3

West	North	East	South
Robinson	Belladonna	Jordan	Avarelli
—	1♠	Pass	1NT
2♣	2♠	3♣	Pass
3NT			

Giorgo Belladonna began with the ♠AK and a third spade. On the second round, Walter Avarelli threw a heart. On the next one, after a pause, he parted with the ◇3. Noting his embarrassment, the commentators predicted that Robinson would draw the correct conclusions and make his contract.

It was not to be. When the clubs failed to break, Robinson put his faith in the heart finesse and went two down. Had his antennae been more sensitive, they would have picked up the message locked in Avarelli's pause when he had to find a discard on the third round of spades. Only with a doubleton diamond would he have been reluctant to part with one. Belladonna, for his part, wouldn't have cleared the spades unless he had hopes of an entry, and what could that be but the ◇K, leaving the ♡Q as the sole honour card to justify Avarelli's 1NT response. With a perfect picture of the distribution, Robinson should have cashed the red aces and exited with his fifth club, end-playing Walter Avarelli.

Not even the best players, and Robinson was certainly one of them, can always rely on their sixth sense.

REFLEXES: AN APPRAISAL

If it were done when 'tis done, then 'twere well it were done quickly.

The speed of a player's reflexes isn't listed among the attributes that distinguish the great from lesser players. Some men, as Malvolio would say, are born with it. A few may acquire it. None can ever have it thrust upon them.

When dummy goes down, declarer and defenders alike should study the prospects carefully, taking all the time they need. Thereafter the rhythm, and more especially a change of pace, may well affect the play.

As usual, let us start with an elementary example:

A Q 10 9 6 5

K 4

Sitting East, you are defending a 3NT contract. Declarer, with no apparent entry to the table, needs to bring in dummy's long suit and, having won the opening lead in hand, leads the knave, partner following with the two. If you win you're lost, so you duck. Of course. But if you pause a fraction of a second declarer will draw the obvious inference and go up with the ace on the next round, felling your king.

It's simple enough — provided that you were ready for it. If, however, declarer plays quickly, before you have studied the hand carefully, you may well be caught off your guard.

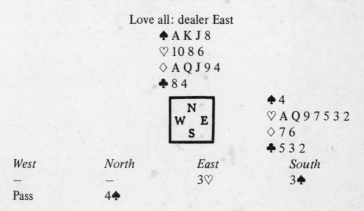

Love all: dealer East

♠ A K J 8
♡ 10 8 6
◇ A Q J 9 4
♣ 8 4

           ♠ 4
           ♡ A Q 9 7 5 3 2
           ◇ 7 6
           ♣ 5 3 2

West	North	East	South
—	—	3♡	3♠
Pass	4♠		

West leads the ♡J. You go up with the ♡A and see South, none other than the great Giorgio Belladonna, drop the king. How do you continue?

The ♡4 is missing. If partner has it and you play the ♡Q – or a low heart, for that matter – you will be presenting declarer with a trick, and maybe the contract. If Belladonna is fooling you, not cashing the ♡Q could be just as fatal. His hand could be:

(a)	♠Q 9 7 5 3 2	(b)	♠Q 9 7 5 3 2
	♡K 4		♡K
	◇A K		◇A 8
	♣J 7 6		♣J 7 6 4

You will have to guess, which means that some of the time you will misguess. Of course, if Giorgio paused even for a second before dropping the ♡K, no guess would be involved. In the event, he had (a) and East, after an agonising trance, misguessed.

This time declarer is Barry Crane, murdered in mysterious circumstances while this chapter was being written. For many years one of America's most successful tournament players, Barry was West in the final session of the Mixed Pairs at the San Diego Fall Nationals in 1984.

♠A K 10 2	♠Q 8 7 3
♡A Q 9 6	♡K 10
◇A J 5	◇K Q 6 3
♣Q 8	♣A 4 3

Barry Crane and Kerri Sherman quickly reached 7♠. Winning the diamond lead in hand, Crane laid down the ♠A, the ♠4 from North, the ♠9 from South. What should he do next?

By playing the ♠K and finessing against North he could pick up the ♠J, despite the 4-1 split. So he did just that only to find this distribution.

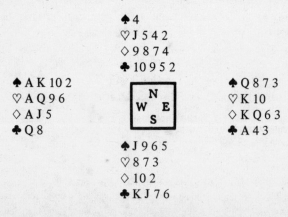

In this situation the ♠9 is a mandatory false card, but it could be a true one, too, so declarer has to guess. He might be influenced by the identity of the defender sitting South. Never having set eyes on him before, Crane assumed, perhaps, that he was unlikely to drop that ♠9 smoothly, as a veteran would do. Anonymity can be a great help.

Long, long ago, in a minor pairs event, I was sitting West on this deal:

Both vul: dealer South

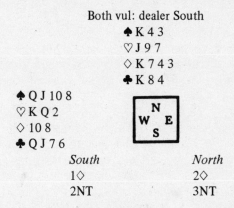

	♠ K 4 3	
	♡ J 9 7	
	◇ K 7 4 3	
	♣ K 8 4	

♠ Q J 10 8
♡ K Q 2
◇ 10 8
♣ Q J 7 6

South	North
1◇	2◇
2NT	3NT

I led the ♠Q which held, and continued with the ♠J, partner following in ascending order. Declarer won in hand with the ♠A and paused at length to study the hand — too long, for it gave me plenty of time to do likewise. A depressing picture presented itself.

Dummy had an absolute maximum for a simple raise. Allowing declarer 16-17, including the four aces, for his 2NT rebid, 3 points at most remained for partner. I could see no way of defeating the contract and was wondering how best to stop an overtrick, when, interrupting my gloomy reverie, declarer led the ◇9. It struck me as an odd card, but without pausing to interpret it, I followed smoothly with the ◇8. I had no Machiavellian plan in mind, but I believe in confusion for confusion's sake, *ars gratia artis*. If partner had the ◇QJ, which was just possible, we had a trick in the suit. If he didn't have the knave, the finesse against the queen would succeed. Either way, what I did couldn't matter.

These were the four hands:

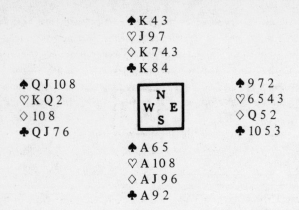

♠ K 4 3
♡ J 9 7
◇ K 7 4 3
♣ K 8 4

♠ Q J 10 8   ♠ 9 7 2
♡ K Q 2   ♡ 6 5 4 3
◇ 10 8   ◇ Q 5 2
♣ Q J 7 6   ♣ 10 5 3

♠ A 6 5
♡ A 10 8
◇ A J 9 6
♣ A 9 2

Since any beginner knows enough to cover the 9 when he holds 108, declarer assumed that I had ◇Q8 or else the bare ◇8. So he went up with dummy's ◇K and continued with the ◇3, covering East's ◇5 with the ◇6. Playing East for ◇Q1052, he lost his cast-iron contract. The result would have been the same had he played me for the double-ton ◇Q8.

He had started with the ◇9, unblocking in advance, to create an extra entry in dummy with the ◇7. No doubt I could have worked it out, but had I stopped to do so the effect of my "impossible" card would have been lost.

Text books say nothing about speed, primarily because it is something which cannot be taught. There's no diagram to depict a sensitive reflex, and yet it's often the key to success.

A situation in *Masters and Monsters* provides a fitting climax to these reflections on speed.

There's a project afoot to handicap the players at the Griffins club. A complication arises when it comes to a new member whose form is unknown. No one on the committee has seen him in action, but one unusual play has been reported and with nothing else to go by, it must provide the basis for his handicap.

♠ Q 10
♡ A K 2
◇ A K Q 8 6
♣ A 10 3

♠ K 2
♡ Q 10 8 4 3
◇ 7
♣ J 9 7 6 5

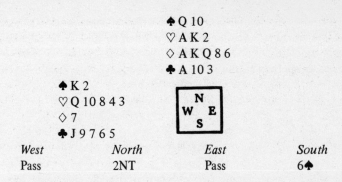

West	North	East	South
Pass	2NT	Pass	6♠

The new Griffin, sitting West, led the ◇7. Declarer won in hand and led the ♠3, to which the stranger followed with the ♠2. On the strength of that card alone the committee had to determine his handicap.

"A far-sighted defence," said Oscar the Owl, the club's Senior Kibitzer. "Declarer is marked with seven spades, maybe eight, headed by the ace, but he cannot have the knave for then he would simply finesse. No, he is clearly trying to guard against KJ2 in one hand. West sees that the defence cannot come to more than one trump trick and that the contract is, therefore, unbeatable unless declarer can be induced to take a wrong view. So he plays low, hoping that declarer will insert dummy's ten and that partner, coming in with the knave, will give him a ruff. To have worked it out, West must have been pretty good."

Colin the Corgi, the facetious young man from Oxbridge, shook his head. "It's far more likely," he said cynically, "that our new member didn't think at all. He just assumed that declarer couldn't have the ace, since he didn't play it, and he was afraid that his king might crash with partner's bare ace."

Unable to agree, the committee decided to consult the Hog, much the best player in the club, if quite the most insufferable.

Having no personal interest, he might, for once, speak truthfully.

"Well," said Oscar, after stating the problem, "is our new member good or bad?"

"It's you who are bad, my friends," replied the Hogg. "Fancy describing a play without mentioning the most important part! How long did it take West to find that ♠2? That's the crux of the problem. If he thought at all, he couldn't hope to induce the wrong guess. So Colin is right and he was afraid that partner might have the bare ace. If he played quickly and smoothly, it was a subtle and daring defence.

Then Oscar is right. But don't forget that the card you play is sometimes less important than the speed with which you play it. The best defence," concluded the Hog, absent-mindedly draining Oscar's glass of Cognac, "is often the fastest."

The fast-thinking player will always enjoy an advantage, but a slower opponent can lessen it by looking ahead, anticipating the problems that arise and pondering over them in advance.

Before playing to the first trick, everyone, quick and slow alike, should pause to think the hand out. Meditate deeply, then play quickly. Admittedly, that is a counsel of perfection. Problems do arise at a later stage, especially in discarding. The answer is to huddle before the need for it arises, while you are still following suit. Without misleading anyone, it will give nothing away. As declarer begins to reel off his spades you know that, say two tricks ahead, you will have to shed a precious heart or bare the ◇K. Decide which it will be before you come to it.

Needless to say, there is one thing you mustn't do and that is to think, when you have nothing to think about, in order to lay a false trail. The slightest hesitation is culpable if it can mislead opponents, but that is something you will not find in the Golden Cupola. For the seamy side of bridge we must go down to the nether regions. *Facilis descensus Averno.* The lift to the basement awaits us.

CHAPTER FOUR

Warts and All

Bridge mirrors every facet of life, and there would be a serious flaw in the glass if it didn't reflect the warts. In the world at large not everyone is scrupulously honest. Why, then, should it be otherwise at bridge?

There is, it is true, a basic difference which makes for rectitude at bridge. The risk of detection is much higher. In everyday life it is debatable whether or not crime pays. At bridge the answer is not in doubt. It doesn't – not because the laws are stricter, but because the offenders cannot get away with it. And there are no suspended sentences, no rehabilitation centres. Drummed out of the club, the miscreant doesn't get another chance.

Cheating as such is virtually unknown – except in the most exalted circles. Among the élite, signalling by seasoned pairs is the usual charge. Some of the best pairs in the world have come under suspicion, not on account of any lapses on their part, but because lesser rivals cannot explain in any other way why they are bested.

"What! They've beaten us again! How can that be? We are the better players. They must have cheated."

Bidding boxes, eliminating intonation, and screens placed diagonally across the table – making it impossible, at least in theory, to measure pauses and trances – haven't put an end to scandal and suspicion. One American pair was accused of overcoming the screen barrier by perfecting a code of coughs and sneezes!

On the international scene and on its fringes it doesn't take much to arouse suspicion. In lesser events, and more especially in rubber bridge, where the unit is the individual and not the pair, secret understandings can hardly exist. And there's much greater latitude. Playing for pleasure, with no cups or trophies but only money at stake, no one is expected to impersonate a metronome or to make every bid sound like a recorded time signal.

THE SOUND OF THE TRUMPET

Cheating does exist, however, in the guise of 'unethical conduct', by way of intonation and hesitation. Worth recalling is an original variation introduced by an old lady of limited ability in the early days of Lederer's club in London. Hard of hearing, the old lady carried with her an ear-trumpet. When she had nothing more to say, she put down her trumpet. An unmistakable sign-off. There was no point in partner making a trial bid for she wouldn't hear it anyway. When the old lady had anything to spare, she kept the trumpet to her ear, indicating what is known as 'an on-going situation'. Since she was a poor player and didn't use her trumpet very effectively, everyone was amused and no one minded.

But let it be said here and now that when good players congregate and the stakes are high, unethical play is virtually unknown. This isn't because strong players are, by nature, more honest than weak ones, but because, just as they know how to draw inferences from the bidding and the play, so they are alive to the information that may be improperly conveyed by every pause and every vocal inflection.

At St James's Bridge Club the ethics are irreproachable. By contrast, at the Royal Automobile Club, where I played for many years, lapses were not unknown. Most of them, though not all, were due to ignorance, and since the mildest complaint only led to unpleasantness, I soon discovered that the best counter was to let the offence boomerang — which it often did.

THE FUMBLE - AND - FLICK

A frequent and much esteemed culprit was a man of wealth, with a reputation in the City which was the envy of Threadneedle Street and Petticoat Lane. He had a habit which I can only describe as 'fumble-and-flick'. When he wanted anyone to think that he had an honour he didn't possess, he made as if to touch one card, then, realising that it was the wrong one, quickly flicked another on the table. It was a slick, artistic performance and worth a lot of points to me over the years. To this day I cherish the memory of a slam I could never have made without the fumble-and-flick.

Opponents having taken a trick, I had to bring in the trumps without loss on AJ76 opposite K1094.

With nothing to guide me I played the ace, then the knave, intending to finesse on the theory that, other things being equal, the queen is likely to be over the knave. With a fumble-and-flick out came a low card. Clearly his partner had the queen, so, playing against the odds, I went up with the king and had the satisfaction of dropping the doubleton queen. It is always pleasing to see the enemy hoist on his petard.

Still at the Royal Automobile Club, I witnessed a particularly gratifying example one day when a notoriously unethical player, with 60 up in the rubber game, opened 2♣. After a pass from the player on his left, his partner went into a long and agonising trance. Finally, looking acutely embarrassed, he emerged with 2♢. Nicknamed the 'Black Prince', East, unlike his partner, was as ethical a player as could be found anywhere. Concluding that the trance showed values just short of a positive response, West, the opener, promptly bid 6♡. These were the four hands:

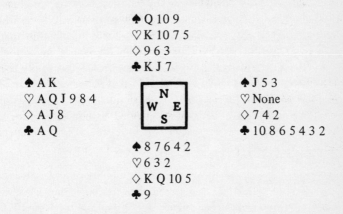

North doubled and collected 1100.

The Black Prince had been torn between the temptation to pass, 2♣ being enough for game, and a stern sense of duty which told him to respect the convention. The sense of duty prevailed and not only was justice done, but it was seen to be done. No one was more pleased than the Black Prince.

HONOURS EVEN

Surprisingly, both parties to an incident, which reflects no credit on either, are apt at times to feel aggrieved. I was once asked to sort out this curious embroglio.

As dummy went down, West, declarer in 6◇, announced: "A 100 honours, partner." East and South duly made the entry on their scoring pads, while North looked vacant as was his custom.

<table>
<tr><td>♠ K J
♡ Q 7 5
◇ K J 10 8 3
♣ A J 2</td><td>N
W   E
S</td><td>♠ A 6
♡ K J 4
◇ A 9 5 2
♣ K Q 10 9</td></tr>
</table>

Declarer won the opening spade lead in hand, laid down the ◇K and ran the ◇J. South produced the ◇Q and before another card could be played a fierce south-westerly gale blew across the table.

West accused South of sharp practice. Seeing the ◇Q in his hand and the ◇A on the table, he knew perfectly well that West couldn't have honours. Why, then, had he entered them?

Why, countered South, had West claimed them in the first place? Each, in turn, professed to have made an honest slip and neither believed the other. The crucial point was lost in the heat of the battle. Why had West finessed against North? If he had made a genuine mistake in claiming honours, should he have taken advantage of the information his error had seemingly brought to light?

How should I have apportioned the blame? Honours even?

THE LADY VANISHES

On a bitterly cold night at Almack's Club the players sat close to a big log fire. It was the last rubber before dinner and West was in a 4♠ contract which depended on not losing a trump. ♠A1076 faced ♠KJ984 in dummy.

West laid down the ♠A, then played the ♠6, North following low both times. Should he finesse or play to drop the queen? While he considered, South turned to bend towards the fire and in so doing exposed his hand. The clubs nestled neatly between the red suits, but nowhere was there any sign of the ♠Q. "Perishing cold," he muttered.

West looked up at him suspiciously and pursed his lips. Then he went up with dummy's king — and brought down the queen.

"That cheat!" he exclaimed after South had left the table. "Did you see how he deliberately showed me his hand, having tucked away the ♠Q, to induce a finesse? Fortunately, I have played with him before."

"That fellow shouldn't be allowed in the club," I heard South saying in the bar a few minutes later. "He looked brazenly into my cards, then dropped my bare queen. It was quite blatant. Disgraceful!"

A DISCOVERY PLAY

An ingenious method of locating a missing queen was reported one day by Jean Besse from a tournament in Deauville.

Playing against two old ladies he had never seen before, an expert found himself in 6NT on:

♠ A Q 8		♠ K 7 6
♡ A Q J	N W E S	♡ K 10 4
◇ A J 6		◇ K 10 9
♣ 10 9 8 3		♣ K Q J 4

A spade was led, taken in hand. Everything hinged on finding the ◇Q, and though technically it was correct to tackle the clubs first, in case it provided a clue to the distribution, declarer, a cynic by nature, thought he could find a better way.

At trick two he led the ♡J and tuned in to the lady on his left. After a barely perceptible pause, she followed low. West rose with dummy's king and, returning to hand with a spade, continued with the ◇J. This time the lady followed smoothly. No suggestion of a barely perceptible pause. So she had the queen. Declarer ran the ◇J and brought home his contract.

All these exploits are taken from real life. The next one is apocryphal, but being much *à propos* provides a fitting pendant to the others.

A K 10 9

7 5 2	N W E S	Q 3

J 8 6 4

South leads the knave. West pauses. East, a strictly ethical player, squirms with embarrassment. Finally West plays the ♠5. Low from dummy — and from East!

"Why didn't you win the trick with the queen?" protests West.

"You thought so long, I though you had it," retorts East with relish.

STRICTLY INFORMATORY

Looking for ladies, if the most frequent, is not the sole source of immorality. Pauses can be no less improper at other times, as in responding to Blackwood.

The least gifted mathematician can quickly count up to four, more especially when the answer is zero. Why, then, should it take any time at all? What does 5♣ mean — after a pause? Clearly this: "I have an ace, but having stretched already, I would rather not show it, officially." Or else the delayed bid is 5◇, the message being: "Very well, I admit it, I have an ace, but I considered concealing it, for my hand will, I fear, disappoint you."

Either way, a pause conveys improper information. A poor player may be unconscious of it. The culprit is partner, if he takes advantage of it.

The same applies with even greater force to a slow double in competitive situations. As South, at equal vulnerability, you open 1♠ on:

♠ KJ10752   ♡ None   ◇ AK3   ♣ QJ96

South	West	North	East
1♠	4♡	4♠	5♡
?			

I wouldn't blame you for bidding 5♠, but should you decide to leave the decision to partner and he meditates before finding a double, you mustn't change your mind because it took him time to make up his. You, not your partner will be the sinner.

A Presbyterian spinster once asked her Minister: "A gentleman told me yesterday that I was pretty and it gave me great pleasure. Did I sin?"

"No," replied the Minister, "there was no sin on your part, but a grave responsibility rests on the gentleman."

Except when they are deliberate, which is rare, intonation and hesitation may be venial offences, but a grave responsibility rests on partner, who must not allow them to influence him.

It has been noted already that inexperienced players are apt to lapse from grace, not through ill-intent, but because they fail to appreciate how an involuntary pause, a gesture, a chance remark, can affect the game. Experienced players know better. But that doesn't always stop them from suspecting others, and that is wholly reprehensible.

About halfway through writing this book I happened to be playing at the St James's Bridge Club with a well-known international from overseas. On my right sat a very experienced player of my own vintage.

"Skip bid, 4♡," called the VEP.

"Skip bid," I repeated thoughtlessly. "4♠".

Of course, mine wasn't a skip bid and of course I should have made the regulation pause. I was in the wrong, utterly and absolutely, and I hastened to apologise. After a pass on my left, my partner, a scrupulously ethical player, reflected, then bid 5♠. Thereupon the VEP objected. The alacrity with which I had bid 4♠ showed that my values were in no way shaded. Quite the contrary. It was all wrong . . .

The VEP had suffered no injury, not yet, at any rate. Above all, he had no reason to suspect that my partner didn't have a full-blooded raise to 5♠ over any 4♠ bid by me, quick, slow or medium-paced. The objection was highly improper.

V.M.	*Overseas International*
♠ A 10 9 6 4 3	♠ K 8 7 5 2
♡ 5	♡ 10 3
◇ A K 8 3	◇ 10
♣ 10 2	♣ A Q J 9 6

Obviously my partner had every right, indeed a duty, to bid 5♠. With a singleton heart I called the slam. The club finesse was wrong, alas, and to paraphrase Lord Acton, not only was injustice done, but it was seen to be done.

Unethical conduct is always deplorable. Accusing others of it, is no less so. The former can be penalised. It's not always so easy to penalise the latter. My partner is still waiting for an apology.

Not cheating isn't, in itself, a virtue. Readiness to suspect others of it comes close to being a vice.

CHAPTER FIVE

Release of the Ego

We are back above ground, but this time on the other, the left side of the Temple, where the faults and foibles and frustrations of *homo sapiens* come into their own. His blunders can be as instructive as his brilliance, often more so. In probing into them our main interest will be, as always, not so much with what he does as with what makes him do it.

How does the ego find expression in bridge?

Alfred Adler, one of the fathers of psycho-analysis, wrote: 'Bridge players suffer from an inferiority complex and find the game an easy way to satisfy their striving for superiority. It offers an opportunity to conquer others.'

Though a gross over-simplification, there's a measure of truth in it. The shortest man can bid as many slams as the tallest, if not a shade more. The elderly spinster can double and redouble as often as the young sex kitten, and feel all the better for it.

For all that, Adler's inferiority complex is only one of the conditions to find expression in bridge. Sadism and masochism, greed and generosity, vanity and humility, all have a place. The schemer, the pedant, the psychologist, the wit, the bore, the law-giver, the anarchist, even the poet, as we saw in a previous chapter, can find gratification in the paste-board world, for as soon as the cards are picked up, the *boutique fantasque* comes to life and over the green baize 'life is real, life is earnest and the score is not the goal'.

In every other game, including chess, the spectators greatly out-number the players. Civilised man, it seems, is too lazy, too weary, too old at any age, to exert himself and likes best to take his pleasures vicariously through the performance of others. Thousands of decadent Romans enjoyed the spectacle provided by a handful of lions and Christians in the arena. Television has turned the thousands into millions, but there's still the same small handful of actors on the stage, be they boxers, footballers or golfers.

The unique feature of bridge is that it's the players, not the spectators, who make up the numbers and set the pace. Everyone is a member of the cast. The cards dictate the script and pick the stars, but every character interprets his part in his own way. Beneath the many-coloured robes the leopard doesn't have to change his spots.

THE BUSY PLAYER

A player's style reflects his ego. To let it roam wild would be prohibitive, but even disciplined veterans allow it to escape from time to time. This is especially true of the 'busy' player, a common type whose lively contours are unmistakable. He is restless, impatient to be up and at 'em, to double speculatively, to pre-empt, to sacrifice, to psyche — in short to do anything and everything except to remain passive and quiescent. Not for him Milton's "They also serve who only stand and wait."

One of the 'busy' player's weaknesses is to double cue-bids and trial-bids. An example, which brought home the lesson to me in the most rewarding way, was a hand I played with Nico Gardener in the Masters Pairs many years ago. Arrayed against us were a world champion with a partner worthy of his metal.

```
                ♠ K 7 5 4 3
                ♡ 7
                ◇ 6
                ♣ A Q 8 6 5 2
  ♠ J                           ♠ Q 10 9 8 6
  ♡ 10 8 4          N           ♡ 9 6
  ◇ A J 10 8 5 3 2  W   E       ◇ 9 7 4
  ♣ 9 7                S        ♣ K 10 4
                ♠ A 2
                ♡ A K Q J 5 3 2
                ◇ K Q
                ♣ J 3
```

At every table but one the contract was 6♡ and, the club finesse being wrong, all the other declarers went down. I was the only one lucky enough to bring home the slam, not through any merit on my part, but solely because East was a 'busy' player. Our auction had been:

V.M.

South	West	North	East
2♡	Pass	3♣	Pass
4♡	Pass	4♠	Dble
6♡			

West led the ◊A and switched to the ♣9. Left to my own devices I would have had to finesse, as did all the other declarers. But East had kindly informed me that he had length in spades, so I had a promising alternative. I went up with the ♣A and reeled off my seven trumps and the ◊K. Reduced to three cards, East couldn't keep the ♣K and three spades. His fatuous double had the effect of executing a *Vienna Coup* against himself!

For another example of an injudicious double 'on the way round' I have selected a spectacular hand from a match between two of Sweden's leading teams in the early post-war days when the Swedes were Britain's most redoubtable opponents in the European Championships. The board led to one of the biggest swings in the annals of first-class bridge.

N/S vul: dealer West

♠ Q J 10
♡ Q 5 3
◊ Q J
♣ A J 6 4 3

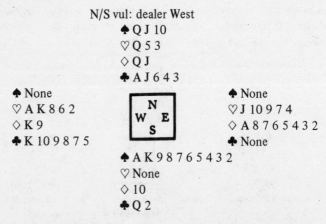

♠ None   ♠ None
♡ A K 8 6 2   ♡ J 10 9 7 4
◊ K 9   ◊ A 8 7 6 5 4 3 2
♣ K 10 9 8 7 5   ♣ None

♠ A K 9 8 7 6 5 4 3 2
♡ None
◊ 10
♣ Q 2

Where husband and wife Einar and Britt Werner, both European champions, sat South and North, the bidding was:

West	North	East	South
1♡	Pass	4◊	Pass
5♡	Pass	5NT	6♠
7♡	Pass	Pass	7♠
Dble			

East's 4◇ was an old-fashioned Asking Bid. When West confirmed the second-round control of diamonds, East invoked the Grand Slam Force, and at this point Einar Werner decided to sacrifice, mentioning for the first time his ten-card suit. He estimated the cost of 7♠ at 800.

Things, however, took an unexpected course. West led the ♡A. Werner ruffed and reeled off nine trumps, squeezing West in clubs and hearts. That came to 2,420.

The action in the other room was even more surprising. Jan Wohlin and Nils Lilliehook, East-West for Sweden, reached 7◇, likewise doubled. During the auction North had doubled West's 5♣ and South dutifully opened the ♣Q. Lilliehook covered, ruffed the ♣A, drew trumps and continued with the ♣10 through North's diaphanous club holding. With the pips working for him he landed the grand slam for 1,580, a swing of 4,000.

North's double of 5♣ wasn't as wanton as West's double of 4♠ on the previous hand. At least he would have welcomed a club lead, or so it looked. He was unlucky. And yet, the question arises: did the seeming advantage of a club lead make up for the information it provided the enemy?

For a pretty example of a fatuous double of a cue-bid — or rather of the use to which a resourceful declarer can make of it — I turn to rubber bridge during the golden age at Crockfords. Sitting South was world champion Kenneth Konstam.

Both vul: N/S 60; dealer North

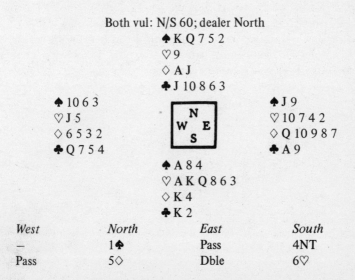

```
                  ♠ K Q 7 5 2
                  ♡ 9
                  ◇ A J
                  ♣ J 10 8 6 3
   ♠ 10 6 3                          ♠ J 9
   ♡ J 5            ┌─────────┐      ♡ 10 7 4 2
   ◇ 6 5 3 2        │   N     │      ◇ Q 10 9 8 7
   ♣ Q 7 5 4        │ W   E   │      ♣ A 9
                    │   S     │
                    └─────────┘
                  ♠ A 8 4
                  ♡ A K Q 8 6 3
                  ◇ K 4
                  ♣ K 2
```

West	North	East	South
–	1♠	Pass	4NT
Pass	5◇	Dble	6♡

West led the ◇2. How should declarer plan the play? The odds against a 3-3 trump break were 2-1, but unless they broke evenly, what would happen to the clubs?

Konstam had the answer. Bearing in mind East's double of 5◇, he won the first trick with the ◇A and ran the ♡9. West won but, as expected, continued with another diamond, and that was that.

Was it really so important for East to ensure a diamond lead? Of course not, but being a 'busy' player he wanted to take some part in the proceedings. Presumably his squeaky double made him feel better.

THE TIME NOT TO BE GREEDY

Penalty doubles fall into a different category, with greed playing a legitimate part, yet some of the same considerations apply.

Not infrequently declarer runs up against an unfavourable distribution and a defender expects, with good reason, to defeat the contract. The temptation to double is understandable, and the busy player finds it hard to resist it. Before succumbing, however, he should ask himself: Will the extra points, if I double, make up for the information conveyed to declarer? Would I still double if I had to expose my hand?

Unless the answers are positive, a raincheck may be the better part of valour.

Dick Lederer, Britain's 'Mr Bridge' in the early days of contract, used to say: "Weak players shouldn't double." The corollary is that it's dangerous to double strong players.

Just as I was about to start this book, I watched Claude Rodrigue play the diagrammed hand. I had an interest, for I was waiting to cut in, so my sympathies were entirely with declarer.

Both vul: dealer South

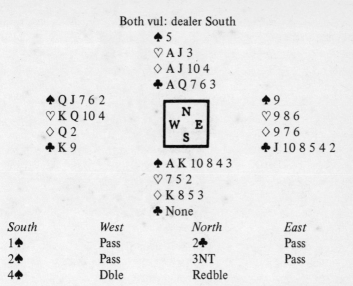

```
                    ♠ 5
                    ♡ A J 3
                    ◇ A J 10 4
                    ♣ A Q 7 6 3
   ♠ Q J 7 6 2                          ♠ 9
   ♡ K Q 10 4          N               ♡ 9 8 6
   ◇ Q 2           W       E           ◇ 9 7 6
   ♣ K 9               S               ♣ J 10 8 5 4 2
                    ♠ A K 10 8 4 3
                    ♡ 7 5 2
                    ◇ K 8 5 3
                    ♣ None
```

South	*West*	*North*	*East*
1♠	Pass	2♣	Pass
2♠	Pass	3NT	Pass
4♠	Dble	Redble	

Seeing all four hands, I felt distinctly frustrated. A heart loser was inevitable, and even if Claude picked up the ◇Q, he couldn't draw trumps without losing three tricks in the process. A bad look-out for us both.

West led the ♡K. Rodrigue went up with the ♡A, cashed the ♣A, discarding the ◇3, and ruffed a club. Next he played a heart. West rose with the ♡Q and switched to the ◇2, dummy's ◇10 winning. The ♡J and ◇A followed, then the ♠A, picking up East's ♠9. The ♠10 gave West his second trick.

Claude couldn't be sure which red card West had left in the 4-card ending, in addition to the ♠Q76, but it didn't matter. If he exited with a diamond to the king, Claude would lead a low trump and score the last two tricks with the K8. If West had the last heart, Rodrigue would ruff and exit with a diamond, again end-playing West in trumps — which is what happened.

I heaved a sigh of relief, for the rubber was up and I could cut in. But would the story have had this happy ending without West's double, warning Claude Rodrigue of the bad trump break?

The odds against a 5-1 break are about 7-1 (14.53 per cent). The double turns it into an odds-on proposition, a warning no declarer would fail to appreciate.

This is another example from rubber bridge at the St James's Bridge club, and this time I was declarer.

Both vul: dealer South

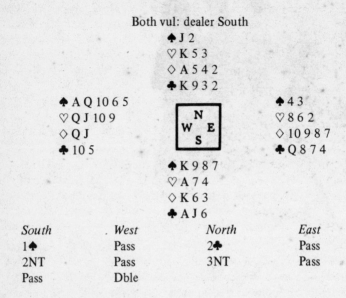

♠ J 2
♡ K 5 3
◇ A 5 4 2
♣ K 9 3 2

♠ A Q 10 6 5
♡ Q J 10 9
◇ Q J
♣ 10 5

♠ 4 3
♡ 8 6 2
◇ 10 9 8 7
♣ Q 8 7 4

♠ K 9 8 7
♡ A 7 4
◇ K 6 3
♣ A J 6

South	West	North	East
1♠	Pass	2♣	Pass
2NT	Pass	3NT	Pass
Pass	Dble		

West led the ♡Q.

There are several ways of going down, and left to my own devices I would have surely found one of them. Fortunately I could trust West. A good player, he wouldn't have doubled unless he had the right cards in the right places, the spades over me and nothing much in clubs — for that, of course, would have been a liability.

I played low to the ♡Q from both hands, won the heart continuation in hand and led a spade to dummy's knave. As I expected from his double, West had the ♣Q and he duly rose with it. A heart to dummy's king followed. This was a good moment to take the club finesse and, not surprisingly after the tell-tale double, my ♣J won. Another spade drove out the ace, and now came West's fourth heart on which I threw a diamond from dummy and a spade from my hand. Six cards remained.

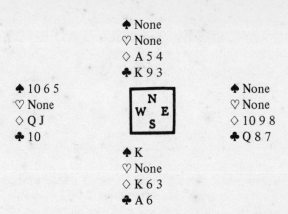

```
              ♠ None
              ♡ None
              ◇ A 5 4
              ♣ K 9 3
♠ 10 6 5      ┌─────────┐      ♠ None
♡ None        │    N    │      ♡ None
◇ Q J         │ W     E │      ◇ 10 9 8
♣ 10          │    S    │      ♣ Q 8 7
              └─────────┘
              ♠ K
              ♡ None
              ◇ K 6 3
              ♣ A 6
```

West continued with the ◇Q. I won in hand and now my ♠K pointed the pistol at East. I could afford to shed another diamond from dummy, baring the ace, but what could East do? If he threw a club, dummy's ♣3 would be a winner. If he parted with a diamond, my ◇3 would be my ninth trick, the two aces ensuring communications. A typical criss-cross situation.

Had West ducked once in spades my life would have been made more difficult. I could have still made my contract, but would I have done so? One thing is certain. Without the double it would have been a case of bad luck rather than good play.

My next exhibit has as its setting a competition confined to non-card playing clubs from which players with more than a thimbleful of master points are excluded. Expertise in such company is not to be expected, but that doesn't rule out common sense or that indefinable *feel* for the cards which is often worth more than mere technique.

Both vul: dealer South

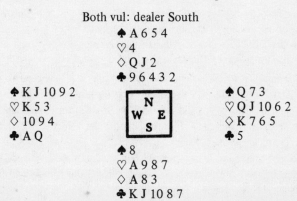

```
                  ♠ A 6 5 4
                  ♡ 4
                  ◇ Q J 2
                  ♣ 9 6 4 3 2
♠ K J 10 9 2      ┌─────────┐      ♠ Q 7 3
♡ K 5 3           │    N    │      ♡ Q J 10 6 2
◇ 10 9 4          │ W     E │      ◇ K 7 6 5
♣ A Q            │    S    │      ♣ 5
                  └─────────┘
                  ♠ 8
                  ♡ A 9 8 7
                  ◇ A 8 3
                  ♣ K J 10 8 7
```

In one room the contract was 3♣.

"Flat board," said South as he gathered his tenth trick. All agreed. This was the bidding in the other room.

South	West	North	East
1♣	1♠	3♣	3♠
5♣	Dble		

West led a spade. Declarer, a lively young lady with scarcely a master point on her escutcheon, went up with dummy's ace and quickly cross-ruffed spades and hearts for the first eight tricks. Next she ran the ◇Q, which held. Seeing Nemesis closing in, West unblocked with the ◇9. The ◇J followed and this time East covered. On declarer's ace West stoically jettisoned the ◇10. If East had the ◇8 the defence would prevail. If not, there was no hope, but it was less humiliating to sacrifice a diamond than to emerge with one trick holding the AQ of trumps over the king. Since South had the ◇8 she made her contract.

"Well played," said West.

"Why, was there any other way?" asked the lively young lady.

Perhaps not, but would anyone have played that way without the double? Had the contract gone one down West's double would have brought in an extra 100. As it was, it cost 750.

How would you set out to make 4♠ on this hand?

Both vul: dealer North

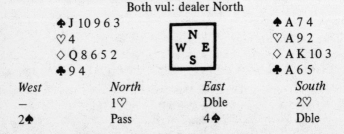

♠ J 10 9 6 3		♠ A 7 4
♡ 4		♡ A 9 2
◇ Q 8 6 5 2		◇ A K 10 3
♣ 9 4		♣ A 6 5

West	North	East	South
–	1♡	Dble	2♡
2♠	Pass	4♠	Dble

North leads the ♡K. You win and rightly play a low spade from dummy. Rising with the ♠K, South forces you with a heart. The natural play without the double would be the ♠6 to dummy's ace and another spade, clearing the way for the diamonds. Alerted by the double, however, you expect South to have four spades, so you couldn't afford a third round of trumps, for you would be forced a second time and lose trump control. And if you didn't play a third trump South would live to ruff a diamond.

To remain in command you lead the ♠J and run it. Let South win. If he plays a third heart you discard a club. A fourth heart would be ruffed with dummy's ace. With the ♠109 intact you would return to hand with the ◇Q and draw trumps. The full deal:

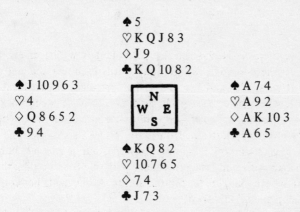

```
                    ♠ 5
                    ♡ K Q J 8 3
                    ◇ J 9
                    ♣ K Q 10 8 2
♠ J 10 9 6 3                        ♠ A 7 4
♡ 4               N                 ♡ A 9 2
◇ Q 8 6 5 2    W     E              ◇ A K 10 3
♣ 9 4               S              ♣ A 6 5
                    ♠ K Q 8 2
                    ♡ 10 7 6 5
                    ◇ 7 4
                    ♣ J 7 3
```

Since North will show out on the second round of trumps you will make your contract anyway if, at trick four, you play the ♠J and not the ♠6. But without the double, would you?

THE CASE FOR REDOUBLING

Redoubles, except the conventional type, are rare in good company and almost unknown in top-level tournaments. In an unbalanced game, they are less infrequent. The reader saw one by North on Claude Rodrigue's hand a few pages back. Vividly illustrating the case against redoubling is this deal sent me many years ago by the great Oswald Jacoby when I asked him for a couple of his favourite hands.

Dealer North
♠ Q J 8 5 4
♡ 5 2
◇ None
♣ K Q J 10 9 8

```
   N
W     E
   S
```

♠ A K 9 6
♡ 6 4
◇ 10 6 5
♣ A 7 6 5

West	North	East	South
—	Pass	Pass	1♠
Dble	4♣	Pass	Pass
5♡	5♠	Pass	Pass
6♡	Pass	Pass	Dble
Redble	Pass	Pass	6♠
7♡	Pass	Pass	7♠
Dble			

'When West redoubled 6♡,' wrote Jacoby, 'I knew that I had been trapped, but I could see that West could not stand prosperity, so I seized the chance to sacrifice cheaply.'

A diamond lead was a gift from the gods. Ozzie ruffed with dummy's ♠8 and led the ♠4, finessing against the ♠6, which, of course, held. The bidding clearly marked West with thirteen red cards and Jacoby made his sacrificial grand slam on an inverted dummy reversal, ruffing three diamonds on the table and using trumps as entries to his hand. His main concern was not to block the trumps, the key play being the ♠8 at trick one.

It was clever of West to underbid deceptively and so lead opponents into an ambush. The redouble was altogether too greedy.

With so much against it, why does anyone redouble? What is the rationale behind it?

Being 'busy' is not the answer. Different motives inspire different players, and the same players at different times. I can enquire profitably only into my own. Why do I do it?

The desire to assert superiority — to conquer others, in Adler's phrase — is perhaps one reason. Another, more compelling, is sheer greed. Assuming that I bring the contract home, I shall win more money if I redouble than if I don't, and playing in mixed company I do not have the same respect for my opponents' judgement as I would in a tournament. Neither do I expect the same accuracy in defence.

There's another, psychological factor at work. The redouble isn't necessarily the sign of an inferiority complex, but it may sow the seeds of one in the enemy. I do not like to be the target for speculative doubles and there's nothing like a successful redouble from time to time to discourage the practice. It's not, however, a weapon for every-day use — unlike the fatuous overcall, which the 'busy' player can use and abuse with apparent impunity, everyday.

RUSSIAN ROULETTE

A penalty at the one level being unlikely, especially at favourable vulnerability, an overcall, however feeble, costs nothing — or so it seems. In fact, unless it's a constructive attempt to wrest the initiative from the other side, it is more likely to hinder than to help. In defence it will mislead partner who will expect values that aren't there. In the bidding it will warn opponents of the pitfalls ahead, or else, providing clues to a favourable distribution, spur them on to games or slams they would not otherwise reach. Look at this deal culled from the records of the 1966 European Championships in Warsaw.

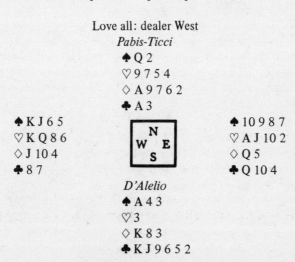

Love all: dealer West

Pabis-Ticci
♠ Q 2
♡ 9 7 5 4
◇ A 9 7 6 2
♣ A 3

♠ K J 6 5   ♠ 10 9 8 7
♡ K Q 8 6   ♡ A J 10 2
◇ J 10 4   ◇ Q 5
♣ 8 7   ♣ Q 10 4

D'Alelio
♠ A 4 3
♡ 3
◇ K 8 3
♣ K J 9 6 5 2

The hand was almost thrown in but, last to speak, Italy's Mimmo D'Alelio scratched up 1◇, the best he could do since 1♣ would have been conventional.

Looking at the North–South hands, with their combined count of 21, one wouldn't expect anything better than a part-score. But that doesn't take account of a busy West. This is what happened.

West	North	East	South
Pass	Pass	Pass	1◇
1♡	2◇	2♡	Pass
Pass	5◇!		

The inferences arising from opponents' bidding revealed a picture in which Camillo Pabis-Ticci could see good prospects of eleven tricks. Clearly, D'Alelio had one heart or none. Therefore he had a second suit. If it were spades he could have mentioned them at the two level. Since he didn't, that second suit must be clubs, and if so, the North–South hands would fit perfectly — which they did.

To this day West probably doesn't realise that he had been playing Russian Roulette. Most of the time his fatuous intervention would do no harm. On occasion, as above, the chamber would be loaded and there would be a loud explosion. At no time could he gain anything except the satisfaction of pulling the trigger.

Weak overcalls have a *raison d'être* in pairs events, where losing 800 may be no worse than allowing opponents to score 110 in 3◇ if you can get out of it for 100 in 3♡. Matchpoint scoring favours the busy player, but with IMPs or in rubber bridge what would be a daring overcall in a pairs event turns out all too often to be fatuous or foolhardy — or both.

THE EGO BREAKS LOOSE

Having learned to master their primaeval urges, champions lead disciplined lives at the table. If they didn't, they wouldn't be champions. On occasion, however, the ego breaks out, soars, and crashes from on high. The greater the champion, the bigger the crash. This was Deal 64 in the 1958 World Championship in Como.

E/W vul: dealer West

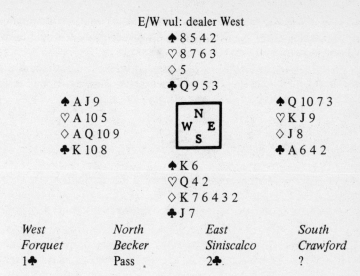

♠ 8 5 4 2
♡ 8 7 6 3
◇ 5
♣ Q 9 5 3

♠ A J 9
♡ A 10 5
◇ A Q 10 9
♣ K 10 8

♠ Q 10 7 3
♡ K J 9
◇ J 8
♣ A 6 4 2

♠ K 6
♡ Q 4 2
◇ K 7 6 4 3 2
♣ J 7

West	North	East	South
Forquet	*Becker*	*Siniscalco*	*Crawford*
1♣	Pass	2♣	?

Pietro Forquet's 1♣ showed a minimum of 17 points. Guglielmo Sinis-calco's 2♣ promised three controls, an ace and a king or three kings.

What would you do as South? What would anyone do? Ninety-nine times out of a hundred any rational player would pass, and maybe the hundredth time, too. Johnny Crawford, described in the *Official Encyclopedia of Bridge* as 'one of the great players of all time', bid 3◇! It cost 1300.

"It's hard to believe," commented Edgar Kaplan who saw it happen.

In the context of a bidding sequence pure and simple, it is, indeed, incredible. As an extravagant escapade by the ego, momentarily released from its strait-jacket, it has its place — if not in Adler's world, perhaps in Jung's or Freud's.

THE ART OF PASSING

Among the figures the visitor will easily recognise in our temple is that of the player waiting in ambush. Unlike the busy player, who cannot bear to pass, passing is his favourite weapon — until the moment comes to pounce.

Guile, and above all patience, are his main characteristics. He doesn't like butting in on threadbare values, pre-empting, sacrificing. He likes to see opponents do it — and pay for it.

The art of passing calls for many skills. Here are some of the artists at work, starting with Pierre Jaïs, partnered by Roger Trézel at a critical stage in a National Pairs Championship at Cannes.

N/S vul: dealer North

```
    ┌───────┐
    │   N   │
    │ W   E │
    │   S   │
    └───────┘
```

Jaïs
♠ Q 8 6 5 4
♡ J 8 6 4 2
♢ None
♣ Q 8 4

West	North	East	South
—	2♣	4♢	Pass
5♢	5♡	6♢	Pass!
Pass	Dble	Pass	6♡

A cold top. At every other table East-West found a cheap sacrifice in 7♢.

Trézel's double of 6♢ was predestined, and Jaïs felt safe in waiting for it. Before he emerged into the open, opponents had to be lulled into a false sense of security — and what could make them safer than the thought that South hadn't bid the slam voluntarily? Clearly it was speculative, so why sacrifice?

No less important than skill and subtlety in ambushing opponents, as Jaïs did at Cannes, is the discipline needed not to be ambushed oneself. Sometimes the trap is set by a cunning enemy. At others it's the work of natural forces and it's up to the wary player not to swallow the bait.

PHILOSOPHER'S PASS

A familiar figure in top-level events is George Rosencrantz of Mexico City, the distinguished chemist who is credited with launching the Pill on an expectant world. He is South here under the spotlight in a pairs event, holding:

♠ AKQJ1076 ♡ K6 ♢ 7 ♣ A92

With both sides vulnerable, West the dealer bids 1◇ and, after a pass from North, East responds 1NT.

Most players on South's cards would double. Some might bid 3♠, which could only be a strength-showing bid in this situation. George Rosencrantz passed! He culd be certain of defeating 1NT by at least two tricks, and he certainly couldn't expect to score 200 any other way. This was the deal:

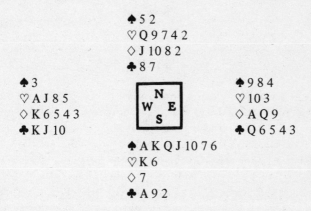

```
                    ♠ 5 2
                    ♡ Q 9 7 4 2
                    ◇ J 10 8 2
                    ♣ 8 7
    ♠ 3                             ♠ 9 8 4
    ♡ A J 8 5            N          ♡ 10 3
    ◇ K 6 5 4 3     W       E      ◇ A Q 9
    ♣ K J 10             S          ♣ Q 6 5 4 3
                    ♠ A K Q J 10 7 6
                    ♡ K 6
                    ◇ 7
                    ♣ A 9 2
```

The defence took nine tricks, an excellent result. It is true, that as the cards are, only a most unlikely trump lead can stop 4♠. But then, unless South shuts his eyes and shoots 4♠ on his own, there's no way of getting there. And why should South shut his eyes?

To quote his partner, Ron Andersen, Rosencrantz was "too good to bid".

With both sides vulnerable, North deals and bids 1NT (15/17). East passes and South calls 2♣. What do you say with:

♠ Q75 ♡ AQ8 ◇ AQJ ♣ AK42 ?

If you double East will assume that you are showing a suit to direct a lead, or else that you have in mind a sacrifice in clubs. So, knowing that North must bid again, you pass. North duly responds 2♡ and, after a pass from East, South bids 3♣. It's your turn again. If you double now East may read it as a take-out double. Do you want him to bid?

Look at the complete deal:

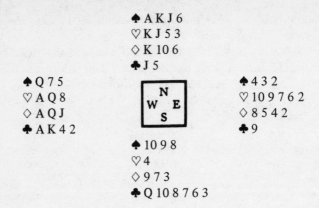

♠ A K J 6
♡ K J 5 3
◇ K 10 6
♣ J 5

♠ Q 7 5
♡ A Q 8
◇ A Q J
♣ A K 4 2

♠ 4 3 2
♡ 10 9 7 6 2
◇ 8 5 4 2
♣ 9

♠ 10 9 8
♡ 4
◇ 9 7 3
♣ Q 10 8 7 6 3

Should East bid 3♡, on the obvious lead of the ♠10 he will go down. If he leaves in the double, which is far from certain, South may go one down. He will if you attack diamonds early on. If you start 'safely' with the ♣AK and a third club, he will make his contract.

You have more than half the strength of the pack in your own hand, yet you can't be sure of scoring more than four tricks in defence or six in attack. Pass stoically.

This is what Michael Lawrence did in a similar situation in the Spingold, one of America's major tournaments.

SAFETY BIDS

The object of every safety play is to guard, whenever possible, against an unlucky distribution. Most safety plays have been standardised long ago, and most players are familiar with the mechanics of most of them.

More difficult to define, and impossible to standardise, are 'safety bids', like those of Lawrence and Rosencrantz on the last two hands. But the basic concept is the same. A player visualises an unlucky distribution and battens the hatches. In play there is often no reason to expect bad breaks, and the safety play is only an insurance. In bidding there may be dire portents for those who know how to read them.

South on the hand below was Claude Delmouly, playing with Omar Sharif against Jeremy Flint and Jonathan Cansino in the famous Piccadilly £1-a-point match, of which more anon.

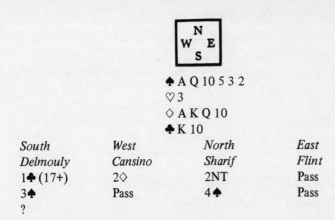

♠ A Q 10 5 3 2
♡ 3
◇ A K Q 10
♣ K 10

South	West	North	East
Delmouly	Cansino	Sharif	Flint
1♣ (17+)	2◇	2NT	Pass
3♠	Pass	4♠	Pass
?			

Cansino's 2◇ was weak, showing length but no strength. Omar Sharif's 2NT promised 10 points or so, regardless of shape. His raise to 4♠ indicated a trump honour. Should Delmouly bid 4NT, enquiring for aces? Should he cue-bid the ◇A or maybe show his second-round control in hearts or in clubs?

Claude Delmouly passed! He reasoned that with a singleton diamond Omar would have made a cue-bid instead of calling 4♠. And if he had a doubleton, Flint was likely to have a void and the opening lead would be ruffed. He had read the situation perfectly.

This was the full deal:

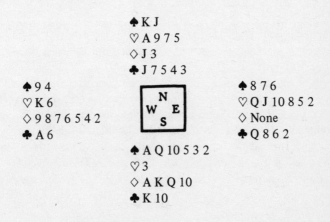

♠ K J
♡ A 9 7 5
◇ J 3
♣ J 7 5 4 3

♠ 9 4
♡ K 6
◇ 9 8 7 6 5 4 2
♣ A 6

♠ 8 7 6
♡ Q J 10 8 5 2
◇ None
♣ Q 8 6 2

♠ A Q 10 5 3 2
♡ 3
◇ A K Q 10
♣ K 10

THE WEAK NOTRUMP

A potent weapon in guarding against misfortune, passing can be no less effective in inflicting it on others.

The ambush element is one of the many attractions of the weak notrump. Since hands in the 12-14 range are not infrequent, they offer many opportunities for lying in wait to trap opponents.

Whenever the opening bid is 1NT, be it weak or strong, the key to the future lies with partner. He holds the crystal. Adding his points to the opener's he knows, and no one else does, which side holds the balance of strength. Opposite a strong notrump anything over 5 points ensures superiority. Having been warned that a powerful hand is out against them, opponents are not likely to intervene on dubious values, so opportunities for trapping them are few and far between.

Not so in the case of the weak notrump. With fewer than 12 points opener's partner has no expectation of game and can pass with an easy conscience. Unable to place a quarter of the pack's strength, opponents cannot tell to which side the hand belongs. If either comes in when the missing strength is with opener's partner he may incur a heavy penalty and save nothing but a modest part-score. If he passes and it's his partner who has the missing values, he may be selling his birthright for the proverbial song.

Sitting West, vulnerable against not, what action do you take when South, the dealer, bids 1NT (12-14)? You hold:

♠ K943 ♡ AK5 ◇ QJ7 ♣ QJ6

It may be your hand. Are you going to let the enemy talk you out of it? Conversely, partner may have nothing and if you stick your neck out, it may cost 800.

Well, which shall it be?

Either way it's a guess, which means that part of the time you will misguess, as did the French West playing against Britain in the 1984 Olympiad. He passed. So did North and East. South took four tricks and lost 150. In the other room, with no weak notrump to confuse the issue, the British bid and made 3NT, scoring 600.

East's hand was:

♠ 107 ♡ Q10842 ◇ AK9 ♣ 752

Interchange the East-West hands and East is only slightly better off. All he knows, if North passes, is that he hasn't enough to raise to game.

He may have more than enough for a vicious double if East comes in at the wrong time.

Vulnerability is an important factor in manoeuvering so as to gain on the swings without losing on the roundabouts.

Special conventions apart, and there are several, the everyday weapon with values deemed sufficient to challenge the weak notrump is to double. This is, of course, primarily a penalty double. When it misfires and opener's partner holds 9 points or more, he redoubles, the signal which says: "We are on top and should be able to double anything they bid."

At equal or favourable vulnerability this is the correct procedure. What if only your side is vulnerable? Suppose that West doubles South's 1NT and you, North, hold:

♠ Q7 ♡ K1073 ◇ 7432 ♣ AQ6

Peer into your crystal. What will happen if you redouble? Opponents will rescue themselves into something and you or your partner will double, expecting a 300 penalty, 500 if you are lucky, a mere 100 if you are not.

And now, say that instead of redoubling you pass. If East takes out the double you will have the same options as before, but West hasn't called on him to bid and even on a worthless hand, with no length anywhere, he will doubtless pass. This time you expect to score 80 below the line, 50 for the insult and 200 for the overtrick, 400 if you are lucky, no overtrick if you are not. All in all, you will do best by passing.

The classical action on your hand is to redouble. At unfavourable vulnerability, don't be classical. Pass.

THE FORCING PASS

Because the busy player so often lacks the discipline to keep his ego in check and to assume a subordinate part when the situation calls for it, the constructive, and at times dynamic properties of the pass should not be underrated. The *forcing pass* is a case in point.

North deals and bids 2NT. East passes and you, sitting South, bid 3♠. West comes in with 5◇ and North passes. So does East.

West	North	East	South
—	2NT	Pass	3♠
5♦	Pass	Pass	?

Whatever your holding you must not pass.

Maybe your values are so shaded that you would have done best to pass 2NT. It's too late now, for North's pass is unconditionally forcing. The inferences are inescapable. If partner has a 21-22 point balanced hand he can certainly double 5♦, but since you know a lot more about his hand than he knows about yours, he leaves the decision to you. With:

♠ QJ752 ♡ 1043 ♦ 6 ♣ Q1065

you double because you do not expect to make eleven tricks, but you do with:

♠ KJ10874 ♡ 10 ♦ 6 ♣ QJ1053

so now you bid 5♠.

Vulnerability is not a decisive factor since partner must have taken it into account when he passed, leaving you to decide.

This is a case of same again only more so. You, South, hold:

♠ 54 ♡ 32 ♦ 5432 ♣ 65432

West	North	East	South
—	—	2♡	Pass
6♡	6♠	Pass	Pass
7♡	Pass	Pass	?

It should take you no time at all to bid 7♠. If North considered that 6♠ would be a good sacrifice over 6♡ it follows that 7♠ would be an even better sacrifice over 7♡. Why, then, did he pass? Obviously, because for all he knew, you might have a trick in defence. Since you haven't, you must sacrifice. Partner has made a forcing pass and you mustn't shirk your responsibility.

Observe that East, too, made a forcing pass over 6♠, suggesting the first-round control in spades. Otherwise he would have surely doubled as a warning to West.

I turn to a forcing pass at rubber bridge. Let's see all the cards from the start and play the hand out.

N/S vul: dealer East

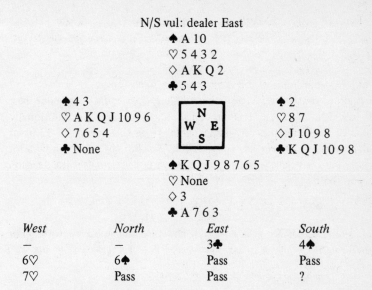

```
              ♠ A 10
              ♡ 5 4 3 2
              ◇ A K Q 2
              ♣ 5 4 3

♠ 4 3                          ♠ 2
♡ A K Q J 10 9 6        N      ♡ 8 7
◇ 7 6 5 4            W     E    ◇ J 10 9 8
♣ None                  S      ♣ K Q J 10 9 8

              ♠ K Q J 9 8 7 6 5
              ♡ None
              ◇ 3
              ♣ A 7 6 3
```

West	North	East	South
–	–	3♣	4♠
6♡	6♠	Pass	Pass
7♡	Pass	Pass	?

Of course North could have doubled 7♡, and I confess that with his hand I would have been tempted to do so, but for better or worse he left the decision to South, inviting him by implication to bid the grand slam. With controls in both the enemy suits South promptly did so.

West led the ♡K and it looked as if declarer had twelve top tricks and no more. And yet, after that bidding sequence, he could have spread his hand and claimed thirteen tricks before playing to the first one! Not being the flamboyant type, he went through the motions.

After ruffing the ♡K he crossed twice in trumps to ruff two more. This was to make certain that, even if West had soared to 6♡ on a 6-card suit, East should have no heart left. All that remained was to cash his winners, eight spades in all and the ♣A. On the last one West was reduced to four cards. Having to keep a heart, since dummy still had one, he let go a diamond. Having served its purpose, dummy's fourth heart was now discarded and the heat was turned on East. Obliged to retain a club, he, too, shed a diamond, allowing dummy's ◇2 to score the thirteenth trick.

A WELL MISTIMED SOS

To make up for the slapdash rubber bridge bidding on the last two hands we will now go over to the 1983 Summer Nationals at New Orleans.

All the dramatis personae belong to the élite, commanding between them, according to the ACBL's *Daily Bulletin*, no fewer than 30,000 Master Points.

Both vul: dealer West

West	North	East	South
1NT	Dble	Redble	?

You are South with:

♠ 9 5 4 ♡ 9 7 5 3 2 ◇ J 10 6 4 ♣ 6

Clearly partner has chosen the wrong moment to step in, but how can the inevitable loss be minimised? South chose the time-honoured device of bidding his short suit, clubs, intending when doubled to redouble for a rescue. Imagine his feelings when North calmly left in the SOS redouble!

This was the deal:

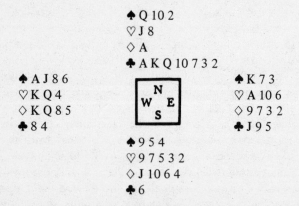

```
              ♠ Q 10 2
              ♡ J 8
              ◇ A
              ♣ A K Q 10 7 3 2
♠ A J 8 6                        ♠ K 7 3
♡ K Q 4          N              ♡ A 10 6
◇ K Q 8 5      W   E            ◇ 9 7 3 2
♣ 8 4            S              ♣ J 9 5
              ♠ 9 5 4
              ♡ 9 7 5 3 2
              ◇ J 10 6 4
              ♣ 6
```

Needless to say, the contract was made.

Some of the ego's escapades go unpunished. Others are expensive. There is one which is *always* expensive — telling partner where he went wrong. The motive isn't so much to make him see the light, still less to improve his game, but rather to assert superiority, to demonstrate that you are the better player. Adler is nearly right, but there is often another reason, too, for berating partner — the need, after a poor result, to absolve yourself of all blame. By proving that partner is guilty you establish your own innocence. The more successful you are in doing it, the more expensive it is, for guilty partners do not give of their best. Experience shows, however, that the ego is usually willing to pay the price.

THE POWERS OF DARKNESS SMILE

To conclude this chapter here is a hand on which, as on so many others, virtue must be its own reward.

E/W vul: dealer South

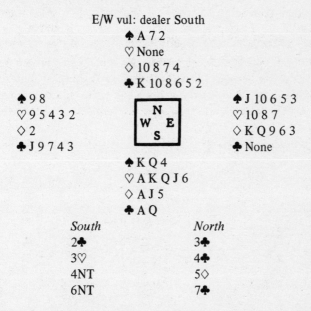

```
                    ♠ A 7 2
                    ♡ None
                    ◇ 10 8 7 4
                    ♣ K 10 8 6 5 2
    ♠ 9 8                          ♠ J 10 6 5 3
    ♡ 9 5 4 3 2        N           ♡ 10 8 7
    ◇ 2            W       E       ◇ K Q 9 6 3
    ♣ J 9 7 4 3        S           ♣ None
                    ♠ K Q 4
                    ♡ A K Q J 6
                    ◇ A J 5
                    ♣ A Q
```

South	North
2♣	3♣
3♡	4♣
4NT	5◇
6NT	7♣

Siting West, you resign yourself, as you listen to the bidding, to paying for 6NT, maybe 7NT. But lo and behold, the much maligned powers of darkness smile on you and propel the enemy into 7♣. You pass gratefully, trying to look nonchalant, and lead the ◇2.

Declarer wins, lays down the ♣A and shakes his head when East shows out. Alas, the powers of darkness change sides, or perhaps they were working for the enemy all the time. Declarer plays off his four top hearts, discarding dummy's three remaining diamonds and the ♠A. A heart ruff and the ♠KQ follow, then a diamond ruff. With trumps only left you ruff and dummy overruffs. Three cards remain. Declarer gets back to his hand with the ♣Q, and whichever card he leads — the ♠4 or the ◇J — you must ruff in front of dummy, where the ♣K10 sit poised over your ♣J9.

Suppose that a novice held your hand. He would have surely doubled 7♣, whereupon South, warned of the bad trump break, would have promptly retreated to 7NT, a contract for which there could be no play at all. In practice, even 6NT would probably fail.

And now imagine that the powers of darkness, treacherous as ever, changed sides again and conveyed to you by occult means what would and could happen. Knowing that 7♣ was unbeatable and 7NT unmakable, would you double the former contract and drive them into the latter?

If the stakes were very high you might just do it. What if they were not, or if the deal came up in a tournament? I doubt if you would emerge as the winner of a battle within yourself, for it is one thing to have a grand slam scored against you and another to be branded as an ignoramus. The pain of the score wears off. The ego remains scarred, and it's the ego that counts.

CHAPTER SIX

Placebo Alley

We haven't left the ego behind us. Far from it, but we now come to a long, narrow, low-ceilinged gallery, unkindly nicknamed 'Placebo Alley', where it finds expression in different ways.

A larger than life oil painting introduces us to the inhabitants in their natural surroundings.

In the centre stands the points-merchant with an abacus in one hand and a computer in the other. By his side, waving flags, is the signaller, weighed down by code-books strapped to his neck. Looking down on them, precariously poised on the bough of a tree, a gaudy parrot, resplendent in blue and yellow plumage, intones raucously: "4NT, 4NT, 4NT."

They are three types of the same species, motivated by the same urge to substitute rules for reason. "I think, therefore I am," said Descartes. The denizens of Placebo Alley couldn't prove their existence that way. None the less, they exist and in large numbers.

THE FADING MIRAGE

In an earlier chapter we saw the points count at its best. Partner opens 1NT, and by adding our points to his we can tell which side has the balance of power and whether our goal should be a game or a slam or a modest part-score. As soon as we leave the notrump zone, however, the point count ceases to be a reliable guide and becomes, at times, a dangerous mirage, beckoning us on with figures which fade away before we reach them.

We can allow to some extent for distributional values. Adding points for every card in excess of four in the longest suit, and another for any side-suit of four cards or more, will help to put the honour cards in their place, but it's a crude yardstick applicable only to moderately balanced hands.

With irregular patterns a good fit cannot be expressed in arithmetical terms and often dwarfs all other considerations. The outstanding example is the legendary Duke of Cumberland hand which has come down to us from the days of whist.

The Duke is said to have wagered a fortune that no one could make thirteen tricks against him with clubs as trumps when he held:

♠ AKQJ ♡ AKQ ◊ AKQ ♣ KJ9

The player who made the bet seated himself over him, as West in bridge diagrams, and took up:

♠ None ♡ None ◊ 98765432 ♣ AQ1042

Dummy was endowed with:

♠ 5432 ♡ 5432 ◊ None ♣ 87653

It was a simple matter to trump the opening lead and ruff out the diamonds, finessing in clubs on the way back.

With 6 points declarer had, in fact, a point to spare. He might have had: AJ876 facing 1095432 in trumps and a void in dummy opposite an 8-card suit. With the missing trump honours split 1-1 a grand slam is there without so much as a finesse!

THE MAGIC FIT

True, you are not likely to hold either of these hands — except, perhaps, on 1 April — but you may well pick up as I once did:

♠ A107632 ♡ 8753 ◊42 ♣ 7

and hear East, on your right, open 1♡. You pass, West raises to 4♡, which North and East pass.

With a mere 4 points you are, by the points merchant's standards, a disaster area, yet you need have no hesitation in bidding 4♠ — with hopes of making it, what's more!

Consider the implications. Partner can have at most one heart and may well have a void. With ten or eleven cards in the minors he might have said something, for he is not altogether without high-card strength. It must be so, for having found a fit, opponents, with 28-29 points, would have been tempted to make a slamward move. It follows that partner is likely to have three spades, if not four. In fact he produced:

♠ Q984 ♡ None ◊ Q9642 ♣ A532

Just enough, but no more than he had 'promised'.

Quite an ordinary affair, you may say, and so it is, but not so very different in principle from the spectacular Duke of Cumberland hand.

Even the best players tend to underrate the magic properties of a fit on distributional hands. South on the deal below was Eddie Kantar, player, author and teacher of world renown. He held:

♠ KQ54 ♡ AQ9743 ◊ None ♣ 542

At equal vulnerability the auction was:

West	North	East	South
–	Pass	1◊	1♡
2♣	3♡	4♡	Pass
5◊	Pass	6♣	?

Kantar writes: 'I hate to admit this in print, but I passed. What I forgot to do was to consider partner's distribution in the light of the bidding.'

North was marked with one club or none, so 6♡ would go at most one down with a good chance of being a make. This was the deal in full:

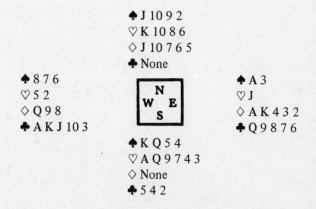

Scant comfort for the points merchant to see an unbreakable slam on 16. In fact, he would probably consider it rather immoral, for he regards counting points as a virtue in itself, like paying one's taxes or saying one's prayers, and would rather go down honourably with the required count than bring home a shady contract on inadequate values.

WHEN POINTS COUNT

And yet the same addict, who mistakes counting for bidding, ignores more often than not the significance of points in the play.

Take up South's cards and make 4♡.

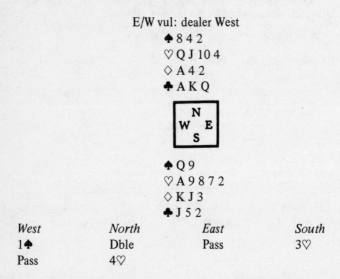

E/W vul: dealer West

♠ 8 4 2
♡ Q J 10 4
◇ A 4 2
♣ A K Q

♠ Q 9
♡ A 9 8 7 2
◇ K J 3
♣ J 5 2

West	North	East	South
1♠	Dble	Pass	3♡
Pass	4♡		

West starts with the ♠K, the ♠A and a third spade to East's ♠J. You ruff, cross in clubs and lose the trump finesse to West's king. A club comes back. Trumps are 2–2 and all follow to three rounds of clubs. Everything depends on the ◇Q. You have no intermediaries and only a one-way finesse. So, do you finesse?

Heaven forbid. West has shown up so far with no more than 10 points and a 5-card suit. To justify any sort of opening he needs that ◇Q. Play for the drop, for you have no other chance. Your prospects, incidentally, are better than they look. Ten of West's cards are known — five spades, two hearts and three clubs. If the three that remain are all diamonds you'll go down. But his hand may be:

♠ AK1076　♡ K6　◇ Q7　♣ 10643

FIND THE LADY

Love all: dealer North

	♠ K Q		♠ 8 5 4 2
	♡ A J 10 9 7 6	**N**	♡ K 8 5
	◇ J 5 4	**W E**	◇ Q 7 3
	♣ 6 3	**S**	♣ Q 10 9

West	North	East	South
—	Pass	Pass	Pass
1♡	Pass	1NT	Pass
2♡			

North leads the ◇K, notes South's two and switches to a club. South wins the trick with the ♣J and continues with the ♣K and ♣A, which you ruff. Another diamond and a spade loser being inescapable, you must bring in the trumps without loss. Do you play for a 2-2 split or do you finesse, and if so, which way? If you try to guess you may be unlucky, so don't try. Make certain of it — by playing a spade. Whichever defender produces the ace, play the other for the ♡Q.

This is the time to count points. North has shown 7 — the ◇K, and by inference, the ◇A. East has produced 8. The ♠A, *plus* the ♡Q, would give either defender an opening bid, 13 for North, 14 for South. Since both passed your *discovery play* can hardly fail.

SIGNALLING

Seen as placebos, signals are in the play what points are in the bidding. They bring comfort and a sense of rectitude, without imposing a strain on the little grey cells. It is so much easier to play high-low, to select odd or even cards or to show preference for a high or lower ranking suit, than it is to rationalise, to infer, to look ahead.

Like counting points, signalling has an important part to play, but it is essentially the means to an end, not an end in itself. To combine the best defence it may be necessary to disclose your hand, or part of it, to partner. But there are times when declarer, not partner, will be the beneficiary. At others, for the defence to prevail it may be necessary to mis-inform partner deliberately, as in this classical example:

♠ J 10 3 2
♡ Q 5

♠ Q 9 8
♡ 8 4 2

Spades are trumps, South having shown a 6-card suit in the bidding. West leads the ♡K. East's *correct* card is the ♡2, but the *right* card to play is the ♡8, followed by the ♡2 on the ace, showing a doubleton. Duly deceived, partner will play a third heart and declarer, with no reason to disbelieve you, will ruff with one of dummy's honours, ensuring a trump trick for you. But for that your queen would surely be trapped.

This is another well-known situation.

♠ 9 8 3
♡ Q 3

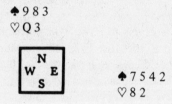

♠ 7 5 4 2
♡ 8 2

Spades are still trumps. Partner starts with the ♡K. The *correct* signal for East is the ♡8, but the right card to play is the ♡2. If you give a come-on signal, then fail to over-ruff dummy, you will give away the trump position and seal the fate of any honour partner may have, maybe a bare king.

A SIGNAL RE-ROUTED

A defender cannot always tell which way the cookie will crumble and tends to do what comes naturally, which is to signal correctly. The diagrammed hand, from rubber bridge, is instructive. I was sitting West.

```
♠ K 4 3 2              ♠ Q 6
♡ A           N        ♡ 7 4 2
◇ A K 4 2  W     E     ◇ Q J 10 9 6
♣ J 8 7 5       S      ♣ A 9 6
```

West	North	East	South
1◇	Dble	3◇	3♡
4◇	4♡	5◇	

North led the ♣2 to dummy's ♣6 and South's ♣K. Back came the ♡5. My first move was a spade to the queen. North's card was the ♠9, South's the ♠8. I ruffed a heart high, crossed in trumps and ruffed high dummy's last heart. Next I played out all the trumps, coming down to this ending:

```
♠ K                    ♠ 6
♡ None        N        ♡ None
◇ None     W     E     ◇ None
♣ J 8           S      ♣ A 9
```

North, who had followed in hearts with the J109, had a singleton trump, so he had to find four discards. He parted with the ♠J10, the ♡K and the ♣3. South, with three trumps, threw the ♡Q8.

Everything hinged on my guessing correctly North's remaining three cards. If he had bared the ♠A I could end-play him by forcing him to lead away from the ♣Q. If he had started with three clubs, the queen would drop. Which should it be?

Had signalling never been invented I would have doubtless gone down, for it seemed more likely on the lead of the ♣2 that North had four clubs than three. As it was, South's ♠8, correct and seemingly innocuous, told me all I wanted to know. North, having shown the ♠J109, South's ♠8 could only have been the start of a high-low signal to show a doubleton. So North had started with five spades and, therefore, three clubs. The queen was bound to drop. These were the four hands:

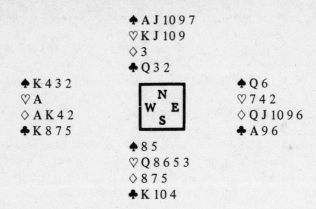

I do not blame South. Most defenders in his place would have played
the ♠8. It was the correct signal and he couldn't tell so early in the
game that it would be re-routed and help me.

A SURFEIT OF SIGNALS

This type of situation arises frequently, not only among the *hoi poloi*,
but likewise in the rarefied atmosphere of bridge at the summit. My
favourite example, which I have used in another context in *The Finer
Arts of Bridge*, goes back to the 1972 Olympiad in Miami. Sitting
North and South were players whose team had won the first Olympiad
for France twelve years earlier. Take up South's cards:

E/W vul: dealer North

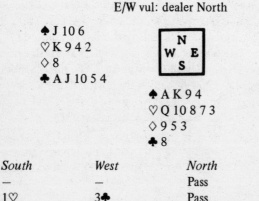

South	West	North	East
—	—	Pass	1♣
1♡	3♣	Pass	3♡
Pass	4♡	Pass	6♣

East-West, Taiwan's Huang and Tai, were playing Precision. Hence the bidding, or rather some of it.

South led the ♠K to which North followed with the ♠2, showing an odd number of cards. South reasoned that it couldn't be three since that would mean that opponents were in a ridiculous slam contract with two top losers. So the ♠2 showed a 5-card suit, and if so, declarer could have no more. South thereupon switched to a club.

This was the deal:

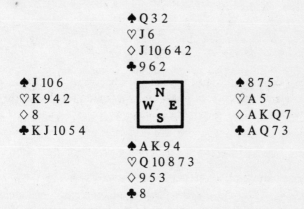

```
                    ♠ Q 3 2
                    ♡ J 6
                    ◇ J 10 6 4 2
                    ♣ 9 6 2
    ♠ J 10 6                        ♠ 8 7 5
    ♡ K 9 4 2          N            ♡ A 5
    ◇ 8            W       E        ◇ A K Q 7
    ♣ K J 10 5 4       S            ♣ A Q 7 3
                    ♠ A K 9 4
                    ♡ Q 10 8 7 3
                    ◇ 9 5 3
                    ♣ 8
```

Truly a triumph for bad bidding over good signalling. Yet I can't absolve North of all blame. Since he didn't want a switch he had no reason to discourage a spade discontinuation, no matter how many spades South had. Through force of habit North gave the right signal, but it was the wrong card to play.

Now for some enlightened signalling:

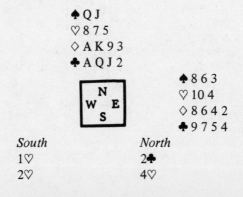

```
                    ♠ Q J
                    ♡ 8 7 5
                    ◇ A K 9 3
                    ♣ A Q J 2
                                    ♠ 8 6 3
                       N            ♡ 10 4
                   W       E        ◇ 8 6 4 2
                       S            ♣ 9 7 5 4

          South              North
          1♡                 2♣
          2♡                 4♡
```

West, your partner, leads the ♠K. What are your thoughts as you gaze, first at your own melancholy collection, then at the awesome dummy? Can you see any hope of defeating the contract? Probably not, for surely partner cannot find four tricks for the defence and you have none yourself.

Camillo Pabis-Ticci, who held East's cards, hoped that in addition to the ♠AK, West might have a trick in trumps. If he didn't, the contract was unbreakable, but no defence should ever be predicated on that assumption. If, however, West had the ♡A or ♡K, he might also have the ♡9, in which case it could, perhaps, be promoted.

Having made his plan, Pabis-Ticci began by following to the ♠K with the ♠8 and echoing on the ♠A with the ♠3. West continued obediently with a third spade, ruffed in dummy. There was general surprise when Pabis-Ticci followed suit, but the message wasn't lost on West. At trick four he was in again with the ♡A and now a fourth spade and an uppercut with the ♡10 promoted West's ♡9 to kill the contract:

This was the deal:

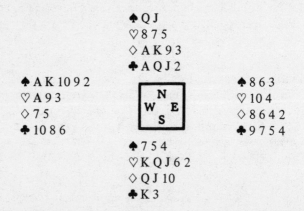

```
                    ♠ Q J
                    ♡ 8 7 5
                    ◇ A K 9 3
                    ♣ A Q J 2
  ♠ A K 10 9 2            ┌───────┐         ♠ 8 6 3
  ♡ A 9 3                 │   N   │         ♡ 10 4
  ◇ 7 5                   │ W   E │         ◇ 8 6 4 2
  ♣ 10 8 6                │   S   │         ♣ 9 7 5 4
                          └───────┘
                    ♠ 7 5 4
                    ♡ K Q J 6 2
                    ◇ Q J 10
                    ♣ K 3
```

Of course, West needn't have had that particular trump holding, but then the signals would have done no harm. Pabis-Ticci was in the heads-I-win tails-I-don't-lose situation and no signals could do better than that.

Does this hand ring a bell? Yes, it's an advanced model of our first example on page 92.

Once more you are East.

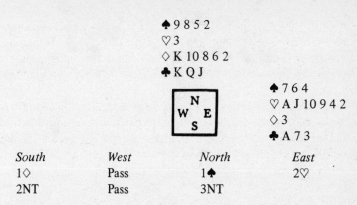

♠9 8 5 2
♡3
◇K 10 8 6 2
♣K Q J

♠7 6 4
♡A J 10 9 4 2
◇3
♣A 7 3

South	West	North	East
1◇	Pass	1♠	2♡
2NT	Pass	3NT	

West leads the ♡7. You insert the ♡9 and lose the trick to South's ♡K. Five diamonds follow in quick succession, then the ♣K. You win and . . . ?

Did West lead the ♡7 from 763 or from Q87? It might be either. Could he have the ♠AQ10 or maybe even the ♠AQJ? That, too, is possible. Either holding will suffice to defeat the contract, but only if you, East, make the right guess, and this is where intelligent signalling comes in. Anticipating your problem, West's first discard when he ran out of diamonds was the ♡Q. Now all was plain sailing. South had:

♠ AJ ♡ K64 ◇ AQJ75 ♣ 1098

but he might have had:

♠ K63 ♡ KQ3 ◇ AQJ75 ♣ 109

Signalling should never be a routine exercise to show strength. Essentially constructive, it should give partner the information — or misinformation — he needs to combine in producing the best defence.

We move to the 1976 Olympiad at Monte Carlo and take the South seat. On our left is Brazil's Gabriel Chagas, on our right his usual partner, Paulo Assumpçao.

North, the dealer, with both sides vulnerable, bids 1◇. You respond 1NT, which becomes the final contract.

♠ Q 4
♡ Q 9 2
◇ A K J 8 4
♣ J 9 3

♠ J 7 3
♡ J 8 6 5
◇ 9 6
♣ A Q 7 5

Chagas leads the ♠K, notes Assumpçao's ten showing four spades and continues with the ♠2, to dummy's queen. You lead the ♣J — perhaps you shouldn't, but that's what happened — and it holds, Chagas following with the ♣10. On the ♣9, which again holds, he plays the 4♣. How do you continue?

Turkey's South, whose hand you are holding, could see seven tricks — one spade, four clubs and the ◇AK. Asking for no more he repeated the 'proven' club finesse.

These were the four hands.

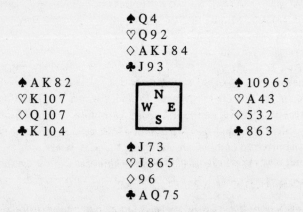

♠ Q 4
♡ Q 9 2
◇ A K J 8 4
♣ J 9 3

♠ A K 8 2   ♠ 10 9 6 5
♡ K 10 7   ♡ A 4 3
◇ Q 10 7   ◇ 5 3 2
♣ K 10 4   ♣ 8 6 3

♠ J 7 3
♡ J 8 6 5
◇ 9 6
♣ A Q 7 5

Chagas pounced and cashed the spades, dummy shedding a heart and a diamond. On play with the fourth spade, Assumpçao played the ♡A and another heart. Chagas ducked leaving declarer to play diamonds from dummy. One down on what looks on paper like an unbreakable contract.

Chagas was a strong candidate for a brilliancy prize. He didn't get it because, as one of the judges later explained, his brilliant defence was only made possible by a blunder on the part of the Turkish declarer. One look at the defender on his left should have told him that a master like Chagas wouldn't wantonly signal a doubleton. South played injudiciously and a brilliancy award should only be made when opponents play well. That was the argument.

I disagree entirely. The best players make mistakes, if only through fatigue, strain, a momentary lapse in concentration. One of the many skills of bridge lies in confusing opponents and taking full advantage of their confusion, whatever the cause. Admittedly, the Turkish declarer shouldn't have fallen into the trap, but had Chagas not bamboozled him, there would have been no trap to fall into.

One final word about signalling. As the last set of examples shows, it can be a powerful weapon. At times no intelligent defence is possible without it. At others it can boomerang. Some cases are clearcut. Others are not. Every one is different, but my advice to you is this: when in doubt, don't. You will win more on the swings than you will lose on the roundabouts.

WELCOME BLACKWOOD

The most widely used of all conventions, Blackwood owes its popularity to its extreme simplicity, and therein lies its greatest defect, for no gadget lends itself so readily to misuse and abuse.

In everyday bridge Blackwood functions as a stepping-stone to slams. And that is precisely what it should never be. The purpose of the convention is to avoid bad slams, not to reach good ones. Having found a fit and adequate strength to make twelve or thirteen tricks, the partnership makes sure that defenders don't win the first two. So they check on aces via Blackwood. Better methods exist to explore slam prospects.

Partner raises your 1♡ opening to 4♡. Holding:

♠ AKJ102 ♡ AQ7654 ◇ 2 ♣ 2

you expect to make a lot of tricks, and yet two aces may be missing. So you bid 4NT, ready to call the slam if partner has an ace and to stop in 5♡ if he hasn't.

Alter the hand slightly to:

♠ AKQ6 ♡ AQ7654 ◇ 32 ♣ 2

Again you want to be in a slam if partner has an ace, so long as it's the ◇A and not the ♣A. The uninitiated, I fear, would still bid 4NT and seek guidance from the ceiling if they heard in response 5◇. The *illuminati* would bid 4♠, hoping to hear 5◇ showing not just an ace, but specifically the ◇A. Over 5♣ they would retreat to 5♡. With the second-round control in diamonds, though not otherwise, North could still call the slam.

Cue-bids, however, require planning. Blackwood doesn't. It can be debauched at will. Hence its attraction. Partner, thrust into a strait-jacket, becomes a zombie. Another attraction.

Let's modify again our original holding:

♠ AKQ7642 ♡ KQJ2 ◇ 2 ♣ 2

Partner opens 1♡. This is the ideal Blackwood situation, for only aces matter. The 1♡ opening could be:

(a)	♠ J853	(b)	♠ J853	(c)	♠ 1085
	♡ AJ654		♡ A7654		♡ A7654
	◇ KQ		◇ A10		◇ A10
	♣ KQ		♣ KQ		♣ A43

On (a) the response to 4NT will be 5◇, so missing two aces we settle for 5♡.

On (b), hearing 5♡, we bid 6♡ and on (c), over 5♣ we call 7♡.

Observe that (a) is the strongest hand in terms of points and (c) the weakest.

Partner opens 1♠. The next player passes. What action do you take on:

♠ AKJ962 ♡ K3 ◇ KQ3 ♣ 8?

Yes, this is the time to bid 4NT. The response is 5◇. Very disappointing, but you have to settle for 5♠.

Do you recognise the hand? You have almost certainly seen it before, for it's one of the most dramatic hands in the annals of bridge. It was the penultimate hand in the 1983 Bermuda Bowl Finals. In a neck-and-neck race Italy were just 8 IMPs ahead, 408 to 400. Bobby Wolff, bid as above and the U.S. scored a game. "No swing," said American supporters dejectedly. In the other room, however, Belladonna and Garozzo landed in 6♡, missing two aces. What, no Blackwood? Well, yes, in a manner of speaking, there was. It was Blackwood as far as Benito was concerned, but not intended as such by Giorgio. The Italians play a sophisticated form of Blackwood, which can mean different things at different times, and so the most brilliant pair in the world, and the most seasoned, had a tragic misunderstanding and the Bowl, so well within their grasp, was lost to the U.S.

It is worth noting that over 176 boards the Americans who bid eight slams and stopped several times in five of a major, invoked Blackwood on only one other occasion. At club level average players would have done it at least ten times — which is one of the reasons they are only average players.

PAINTING LILIES

It was said of Austria's Willy Frischauer, one of the most brilliant card players of the day, that he overbid deliberately, not because he didn't know any better, but because it was unworthy of his skill to bring home easy contracts. He owed it to himself to make them difficult. Similarly, many experts want an ace-locating apparatus, but disdain simple Blackwood as being beneath their dignity.

Several schemes are in use for painting the lily. There's Roman Blackwood in which a 5♡ response shows two aces of the same rank and colour, 5♠ two aces of unlike rank and colour. Key-card Blackwood, also an improvement, treats the king of trumps as an ace. Another adaptation is to respond 5♣ with all four aces or none. Since no expert could misplace four aces, there can be no question of mistaking one response for the other — in theory. In practice it has happened more than once, notably in the world championship in Taipeh in 1971, when the French, playing an unaccustomed formation, bid a grand slam under the impression that they had all four aces. A regrettable oversight. They had none.

Playing key-card Blackwood, a highly experienced American pair in the 1975 world championship reached 7♠ without the ace of trumps. In Stockholm, in 1983, another pair of American veterans, having pinpointed with deadly accuracy all the lesser features, arrived at 7♡ missing two aces and the king of trumps.

These are among the many exhibits of extravaganza by world players detailed in *The Other Side of Bridge*. If I recall them here it is to reinforce my earlier warning. For the average player Blackwood is too simple, too readily available as a thought-substitute, so he uses it too often. But take heed of the calamaties which have befallen the

champions. Don't make it too difficult. The worst time for misunder-
standings is at the slam level.

INTERCEPTION

As with all signals and conventions, Blackwood messages can be inter-
cepted and put to good use against the senders.

Many years ago, at the Royal Automobile Club, I sat West on the
deal below:

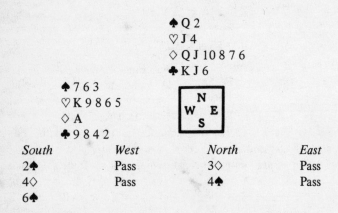

	♠ Q 2		
	♡ J 4		
	◇ Q J 10 8 7 6		
	♣ K J 6		

♠ 7 6 3
♡ K 9 8 6 5
◇ A
♣ 9 8 4 2

South	*West*	*North*	*East*
2♠	Pass	3◇	Pass
4◇	Pass	4♠	Pass
6♠			

I led a heart hoping to set up a trick to cash when I came in with the
◇A. East covered dummy's knave with the queen, and declarer's ace
won the trick. Three rounds of trumps followed. East, with one spade,
threw the ♣10, then the ♣3. My ◇A won the fifth trick and I was left
with a guess — should I play a club to partner's ace or try to cash
my ♡K?

I have always regarded bad guessing as one of the worst faults at
bridge and had I misguessed on this occasion I should never have
forgiven myself. Declarer couldn't have a club. Missing two aces —
diamonds and clubs — he would have applied Blackwood. He didn't.
That was an unmistakable clue. His hand was:

♠ AKJ10984 ♡ A2 ◇ K954 ♣ None

Freak hands make a mockery of formulae, points, honours, even aces.
This curio from *Australian Bridge* is a good example.

E/W vul: dealer North

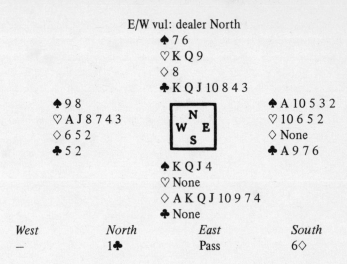

♠ 7 6
♡ K Q 9
◇ 8
♣ K Q J 10 8 4 3

♠ 9 8
♡ A J 8 7 4 3
◇ 6 5 2
♣ 5 2

♠ A 10 5 3 2
♡ 10 6 5 2
◇ None
♣ A 9 7 6

♠ K Q J 4
♡ None
◇ A K Q J 10 9 7 4
♣ None

West	North	East	South
—	1♣	Pass	6◇

Defenders have aces in three suits, but if any one of them is played to the first trick the contract can't be beaten. Only a trump lead will do that.

Declarer has a losing spade, in addition to the ace, and if either a heart or a club is led a trick is set up immediately in dummy, with the ◇8 providing the entry. What if West leads the ♣9 and East ducks? As the cards are, all declarer need do is to continue with a spade honour. Having no trump, East can't remove dummy's ◇8 and the ♠4 will be ruffed.

PLUS ÇA CHANGE...

As we come to the end of Placebo Alley we cannot help contrasting the ways of the inhabitants with those of the busy, aggressive players in the last chapter. They are opposites, or seem to be. Yet they have one salient feature in common. Both find in bridge a happy medium for self-expression. If the one suffers from an inferiority complex, as Adler would have it, the other is basically insecure and looks to rules and regulations, formulae and tables to provide the safety for which his nature craves. So long as his bidding is in line with his points and his play with the signals, he can hold his head high, secure in the knowledge that he has done the right thing — even if it has led to the wrong result.

Away from the bridge table, the points-signals-Blackwood addict is probably a civil servant. If he isn't, he should be.

It is so much easier to follow the regulations than to take the initiative, to obey orders than to accept responsibility. To avoid thinking,
when a substitute is available, is a temptation many humans cannot
resist, and bridge players, even champions, are essentially human —
which is why the game is so fascinating. Oscar Wilde complained that
he could go for a whole day without coming across a single temptation
to which he could succomb. Had he played bridge he would have been
spared this privation.

CHAPTER SEVEN

Rubber Bridge and Duplicate

Having seen the bridge player in all his guises, at his best and at his worst, sometimes inspired, sometimes crude, in which medium would you like to express yourself — money, matchpoints or IMPs?

Each, in turn, has something to offer which the others lack, but there's a radical difference between tournament and rubber bridge. It isn't the scoring or the general standard, so much as the partnership factor, which operates in very different ways.

In all forms of duplicate the unit is the pair. In the money game it is the individual. In teams or pairs events you play with your favourite partner. At rubber bridge your partner is often your favourite opponent. You are no longer on the flat. It's an obstacle race with risks and hazards which make for excitement deal after deal — too much for some. But then, as Harry Truman said: "If you can't stand the heat don't come into the kitchen." If you want a quiet life, stick to duplicate.

THE STAKES AND THE STANDARD

It is widely believed that the standard is far higher in duplicate than in rubber bridge. That is a gross over-simplification. Admittedly, in the family circle, bidding and play are on a rough-and-ready basis. But that applies in equal measure to tennis and to chess, to the violin and the piano. It's the setting, not the type of game or the nature of the instrument, which conditions the performance.

The keen, ambitious players soon leave home and make for the wide open spaces, first the schools, then the clubs, and finally the tournaments.

In club bridge the standard depends on the stakes. Where they are high, so, by and large, is the standard. Many internationals regularly play for money, but I have yet to see one playing for peanuts.

No player past or present has greater claims to immortality than

Howard Schenken, 'the experts' expert'. Three times world champion, a winner, again and again, of all the cups and trophies America has to offer, Schenken hands could fill a book. Yet you would find none to surpass this gem from rubber bridge, voted at the time as the prettiest hand of the year.

Vulnerable and with a part-score of 60, Howard Schenken sat South.

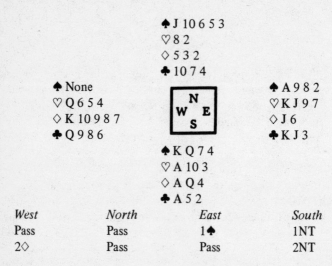

	♠ J 10 6 5 3	
	♡ 8 2	
	◇ 5 3 2	
	♣ 10 7 4	

♠ None   ♠ A 9 8 2
♡ Q 6 5 4   ♡ K J 9 7
◇ K 10 9 8 7   ◇ J 6
♣ Q 9 8 6   ♣ K J 3

                 ♠ K Q 7 4
                 ♡ A 10 3
                 ◇ A Q 4
                 ♣ A 5 2

West	North	East	South
Pass	Pass	1♠	1NT
2◇	Pass	Pass	2NT

The part-score explains the bidding, but the point of the hand is in the play. West led a diamond to the knave and queen. Schenken could see seven tricks, three spades, two diamonds, and two other aces. But where could he find an eighth trick? East, Sam Fry, a player of renown, would surely hold up his ♠A till the fourth round, so what hope was there? Any ideas?

Schenken found the solution, brilliant in its simplicity. At trick two he led the ◇4!

West, with two possible entries, returned the suit and Sam Fry had to find a discard. He let go the ♠2, and who could blame him? After all, with a spade in his hand West would have played exactly the same way and Fry had no other card readily available.

Schenken had done nothing complicated, but he found the one way in which his opponent could be induced to make the wrong guess.

Adam Meredith, one of Britain's few world champions, a professional without prefix or suffix, played money bridge daily at Lederer's Club. His brilliance in tournaments brought him many tributes. He was no less brilliant at Lederer's, but there was no one, alas, to record it.

> Many a gem of purest ray serene
> Unfathomed caves of ocean bear.

I owe this example to Derek Rimington's *Learn Bridge from the Experts*.

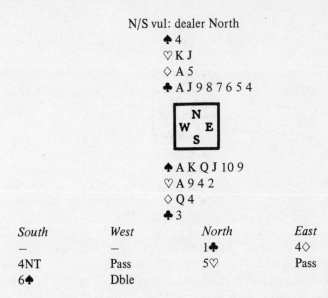

N/S vul: dealer North

```
            ♠ 4
            ♡ K J
            ◇ A 5
            ♣ A J 9 8 7 6 5 4

                 N
               W   E
                 S

            ♠ A K Q J 10 9
            ♡ A 9 4 2
            ◇ Q 4
            ♣ 3
```

South	West	North	East
—	—	1♣	4◇
4NT	Pass	5♡	Pass
6♠	Dble		

East's pre-empt ruled out scientific investigation but Meredith refused to be shut out, and finding partner with two aces, bid a speculative slam.

West led the ♣K to dummy's ace on which East threw the ◇10. How can declarer come to twelve tricks?

East's failure to ruff the ♣A marked him with an all-red hand and that allowed Meredith's vivid imagination to conjure up a distribution that would make it possible to bring home a seemingly impossible slam.

West had to have the ♡Q10x, but how could Meredith get back to his hand to draw trumps? If he ruffed a club he wouldn't have enough trumps left to draw West's, who had six — since West had none.

Meredith's answer was to discard the ◇A on one of his trumps! After six rounds of trumps he took the fateful heart finesse, cashed the ♡K and exited with the ◇5, forcing East to return a red card.

Observe that unless the ◇A is jettisoned, East is in no trouble. This was the deal:

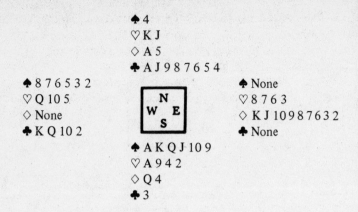

♠ 4
♡ K J
◇ A 5
♣ A J 9 8 7 6 5 4

♠ 8 7 6 5 3 2
♡ Q 10 5
◇ None
♣ K Q 10 2

N
W   E
S

♠ None
♡ 8 7 6 3
◇ K J 10 9 8 7 6 3 2
♣ None

♠ A K Q J 10 9
♡ A 9 4 2
◇ Q 4
♣ 3

FLASHBACK TO AUCTION

One of the most dramatic hands in rubber bridge goes back to the days
of Auction, when you scored whatever you made, not what you bid,
and so long as you gathered thirteen tricks you would earn your bonus
for a grand slam, as well as for the game, even if your contract were a
lowly 1♣ or 1◇. The concept of vulnerability didn't exist.

Signalling was in its infancy, and the margin of error in defence
often made the result unpredictable until the end. Doubles and redoubles,
flashing across the table freely, added to the excitement.

The scene was London's famous Portland Club, the most ancient
and the most exclusive in the world, and the most authoritative, remaining to this day one of the three bodies which, with the European and
American Bridge Leagues, promulgate the Laws of Contract Bridge.

Dealer West

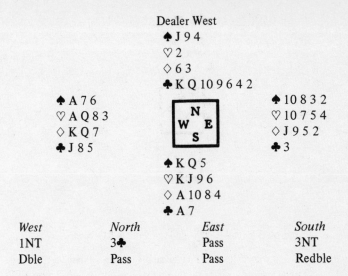

♠ J 9 4
♡ 2
◇ 6 3
♣ K Q 10 9 6 4 2

♠ A 7 6
♡ A Q 8 3
◇ K Q 7
♣ J 8 5

♠ 10 8 3 2
♡ 10 7 5 4
◇ J 9 5 2
♣ 3

♠ K Q 5
♡ K J 9 6
◇ A 10 8 4
♣ A 7

West	North	East	South
1NT	3♣	Pass	3NT
Dble	Pass	Pass	Redble

West made the conventional lead of the ♡3 which declarer won deceptively with the ♡K. Next he laid down the ♣A, and simulating a singleton, continued with the ♣K and ♣Q to create the impression that he hoped to find in the ♠J an entry to dummy's clubs.

West duly held off and now, to his dismay, South produced the ♣7. Discarding wasn't easy, but at least he 'knew' that East had the ♡J, so in the 3-card ending he kept the ♠A and ◇KQ. The sight of the ♡J in South's hand came as a nasty shock. Thoroughly unnerved, West parted with the ♠A to retain ◇KQ, allowing declarer to score all thirteen tricks.

I have seen this hand presented in different settings, and strictly without acknowledgements, more than once in the bridge media overseas. I believe that it was first recorded in print by Edward Mayer, for many years the bridge correspondent of *The Times*, in a book review.

With signalling a universal practice, it couldn't quite happen today, but the panache, the dare-devil spirit, which it epitomises can still be found in the money game — especially after a good dinner, a rarity, alas, in the tournament world.

FLIRTING WITH FORTUNE

Both vul: dealer North

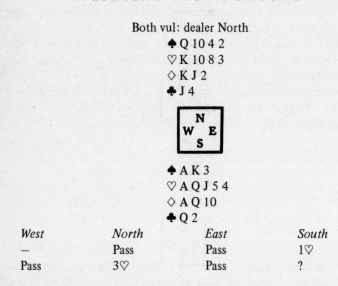

♠ Q 10 4 2
♡ K 10 8 3
◇ K J 2
♣ J 4

♠ A K 3
♡ A Q J 5 4
◇ A Q 10
♣ Q 2

West	North	East	South
–	Pass	Pass	1♡
Pass	3♡	Pass	?

What should you bid? And next, seeing the two hands, in which contract would you like to play?

To take the second question first, the obvious answer is 4♡. Can
there, indeed, be any other? I suggest that an iconoclastic 6♡ would
be a more desirable contract, one, that is, which would succeed most
of the time and should, therefore, be bid.

Consider the likely course of events. Unless West has both the top
honours in clubs he will have no reason to lead the suit. There are
three others to choose from, with trumps having the edge, and without
a club lead the odds are surely in declarer's favour. The spade finesse,
even money, will allow him to dispose of a club loser, and if the suit
breaks 4–2 the knave may drop. Besides, in the end-game the diagnosis
may point to a 3–3 break.

All in all, you have good prospects of making 6♡. But there is one
important proviso – that the bidding has given nothing away. If you
launch into cue-bids, you will inevitably pinpoint the club position.
So, knowing of your two club losers, you will stay in 4♡, maybe 5♡,
and miss a likely slam.

When I picked up the South hand, at the St James's Bridge Club,
my joy at the sight of so many high cards was quickly muted by the
difficulty I found in bidding them. The shape didn't justify a 2♡ bid.

The overall strength fell just short of 2♣. So I bid 1♡ and was promptly confronted by another, no less thorny, problem when partner found an unexpected raise to 3♡.

Surely, I thought, there must be a slam here. But how could I find out? If I bid 3♠, would partner show me a singleton club, or the ♣K, for that matter?

After carefully weighing the imponderables, I bid — or should I say, shot — 6♡. The sight of dummy confirmed my fears. The trump lead raised my hopes.

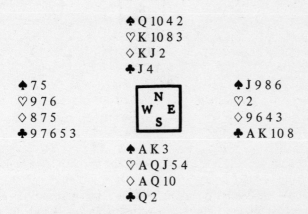

```
              ♠ Q 10 4 2
              ♡ K 10 8 3
              ◊ K J 2
              ♣ J 4
  ♠ 7 5                        ♠ J 9 8 6
  ♡ 9 7 6          N           ♡ 2
  ◊ 8 7 5      W       E       ◊ 9 6 4 3
  ♣ 9 7 6 5 3      S           ♣ A K 10 8
              ♠ A K 3
              ♡ A Q J 5 4
              ◊ A Q 10
              ♣ Q 2
```

As you can see, the spade finesse would have lost, the knave was well-guarded and the suit didn't break 3-3. For all that, the slam materialised by itself. My eighth red winner reduced East to five cards. To keep four spades — if West had the ♠K I would go down anyway — he was forced to shed the ♣K. Now a club brought me my twelfth trick — and a good slam reached by 'bad' bidding.

The lesson to be learned is that the merits of a contract depend in large measure on how it is reached. At rubber bridge simple, direct methods are best, if only because so many partners might misinterpret others.

What of duplicate? Wouldn't top-class tournament players feel ashamed to end up in a slam with two top losers? Wouldn't they, like Molière's doctors, prefer to see a patient die, after prescribing the correct treatment, than cure him by shady, unorthodox means?

I know of no better example than this deal in the trials held to select the American team in 1963. With match-point scoring, pairs events determined the selection.

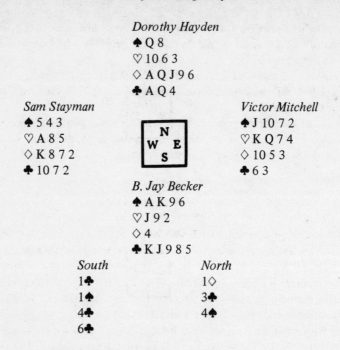

Dorothy Hayden
♠ Q 8
♡ 10 6 3
◇ A Q J 9 6
♣ A Q 4

Sam Stayman
♠ 5 4 3
♡ A 8 5
◇ K 8 7 2
♣ 10 7 2

Victor Mitchell
♠ J 10 7 2
♡ K Q 7 4
◇ 10 5 3
♣ 6 3

B. Jay Becker
♠ A K 9 6
♡ J 9 2
◇ 4
♣ K J 9 8 5

South	North
1♣	1◇
1♠	3♣
4♣	4♠
6♣	

With no stop in hearts 3NT didn't look attractive, and once the partner-ship was committed to clubs it was worth the extra risk to bid the slam. Such is the rationale of matchpoint scoring.

What should West lead?

Put yourself in Sam Stayman's position. Having bid three suits, Dorothy Hayden was 'marked' with a singleton heart or none. A diamond, forcing declarer to take a finesse decision before she was ready, seemed the best bet. Sam Stayman duly led a diamond.

One look at dummy, and Becker quickly recognised an all-or-nothing situation. Everything had to be right — and more besides. He finessed the ◇Q, cashed the ace, ruffed a diamond, crossed to the queen of trumps and ruffed another. Barely pausing for breath, Becker drew trumps — ending in dummy — and cashed the fifth diamond, bringing about this 5-card ending.

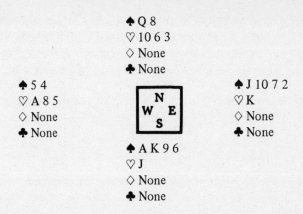

♠ Q 8
♡ 10 6 3
◇ None
♣ None

♠ 5 4
♡ A 8 5
◇ None
♣ None

♠ J 10 7 2
♡ K
◇ None
♣ None

♠ A K 9 6
♡ J
◇ None
♣ None

To keep four spades, Victor Mitchell, East, had to bare his ♡K and since his last discard was the ♡Q, his distribution presented no mystery.

Becker led the ♠Q, then the ♠8, intending to run it if he was given the chance. Wide awake, Victor Mitchell went up with the ♠10, and now, winning with the ♠K, B. Jay Becker produced one of the most remarkable end-plays in the annals of bridge.

With three cards remaining, he led the ♡J. If Stayman allowed the trick to run up to Mitchell's ♡K, he would be end-played in spades. If Stayman went up with the ♡A he would himself be end-played in hearts.

Of course, pointed out Freddie Sheinwold in a light-hearted commentary, had the six and five of hearts been transposed, Stayman would have had no problem — and Becker would have had no hope. That, no doubt, added Sheinwold, was where Dorothy's feminine intuition came in. Something must have told her that the ♡6 was a vital card. With the ♡5 in its place she would have surely settled for the inferior contract of 3NT.

As long as the balance of confusion is with declarer, he need not strive for too much science.

THE PARTNER SYNDROME

A distinctive feature of rubber bridge is the unbalanced nature of the game. Often a moment of tension, the cut for partners can be decisive for with every rubber the cardinal points change their colour. You do not bid the hand the same way on Tuesday as you would have done on Monday, for West and North have changed places and the compass points in a different direction. Neither will you play the same way on Friday as you did on Thursday, when sitting East is the lady who was West the day before.

Protecting weak partners, making the most of strong ones, taking account of the idiosyncrasies of each player in turn — that is the everyday currency of the money game, for which matchpoints and IMPs provide no equivalent.

THE PERILS OF A FIT

With both sides vulnerable and a part-score of 60 to the enemy, West deals and bids 1♠. North passes and East raises to 2♠. Two more passes follow. Now partner, an intrepid lady who doesn't like to go quietly, looks at the score, then at the ceiling, then again at the score, and finally doubles. East passes. What action do you take on?

♠ J9763 ♡ 62 ◇ 543 ♣ 965

That was my hand and I began to count the cost while partner was still looking at the ceiling. By the time the double came round to me I would have settled for £40 — 800 at £5 a hundred. But would I get the chance? If I bid 3♣ or 3◇ I would be almost certain to run into a 4-card fit and if opponents bid on, so would partner. How could I stop her?

The thought of a craven pass flitted through my mind but that would have led to the biggest penalty of all, not on this hand, but on many others that I would play with the intrepid lady over the years. Distrusting me for ever more, she would bid my hand without giving me a chance to apply the brakes.

Suddenly I had an inspiration. What would partner like to hear least? Without a doubt, 2NT — a wanton, destructive bid which could not fail to depress her. So I promptly bid 2NT, still clinging to the hope of getting out of it for £40.

Expecting me, apparently, to have a two-suiter in the minors, West decided to take the rubber and much to my relief called 3♠. The deal was:

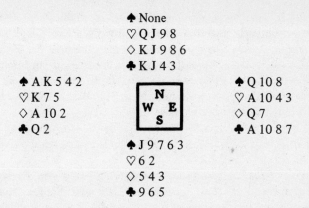

```
                    ♠ None
                    ♡ Q J 9 8
                    ◇ K J 9 8 6
                    ♣ K J 4 3
   ♠ A K 5 4 2          N          ♠ Q 10 8
   ♡ K 7 5         W       E       ♡ A 10 4 3
   ◇ A 10 2            S           ◇ Q 7
   ♣ Q 2                           ♣ A 10 8 7
                    ♠ J 9 7 6 3
                    ♡ 6 2
                    ◇ 5 4 3
                    ♣ 9 6 5
```

The contract went one down. Partner, without quite knowing what happened, forgave me. Better still, opponents were at loggerheads, always a profitable pastime.

If West wouldn't double himself, why couldn't he pass it round to East?

If East was so anxious to double, why didn't he redouble in the first place? How was West to know?

DOES IT PAY TO BE CLEVER?

Neither side is vulnerable and East–West have a part-score of 30. East and South are experts. North and West are making them up:

```
                    ♠ K J 10 5
                    ♡ J 10
                    ◇ 6 3
                    ♣ K 9 7 5 2
                        N           ♠ Q 2
                    W       E       ♡ 8 6 4
                        S           ◇ Q 10 9 8 7
                                    ♣ A Q 10
```

West	North	East	South
1NT (12–14)	Pass	Pass	2♡
Pass	Pass	3◇	Pass
Pass	3♡	Pass	Pass
4◇	Pass	Pass	4♡
Dble			

West cashed the ◇AK and switched to the ♡5, dummy's ♡10 winning.
Declarer took stock and continued with the ♣K. What could it mean?

Surely he couldn't be trying to set up the clubs? Besides, if that was
his idea, why not play up to the king? Could he be cutting communications? Preparing a re-entry? It seemed utterly implausible. The only
rational explanation was — a *Discovery Play*. West's 1NT was limited
to 14 points, so he couldn't have both black aces in addition to the
◇AK. But he needed one of them, so before broaching the spades
declarer would want to know where the honours were. His pattern
was almost certainly 5-6-2-0.

Playing smoothly, with no tell-tale pause that could betray his
holding, East followed to the ♣K with the ♣10. South would ruff,
needless to say and, placing West with the ♣A and East with the ♠A,
he would finesse the ♠10. East congratulated himself on a pretty
defence. How do I know? Because I was East. Imagine the shock
when South, who couldn't possibly have a club, as I had proved con-
clusively, followed with the ♣3!

```
              ♠ K J 10 5
              ♡ J 10
              ◇ 6 3
              ♣ K 9 7 5 2

  ♠ A 4           N          ♠ Q 2
  ♡ 7 5 2      W     E       ♡ 8 6 4
  ◇ A K J 4       S          ◇ Q 10 9 8 7
  ♣ J 8 6 4                  ♣ A Q 10

              ♠ 9 8 7 6 3
              ♡ A K Q 9 3
              ◇ 5 2
              ♣ 3
```

Having brought off a spectacular swindle, South could afford to be
generous. "I was lucky," he said, turning towards me, "to be up against
an opponent who knows all the tricks of the trade and, of course, to
find you with both the ace and queen of clubs. That did make it
'impossible' for me to have a club."

I vowed vengeance.

Soon after, in another encounter with the same clever player, I was
South and he was East. His partner was 'fair-to-middling'. Mine could
never aspire to third-class status. He both overbid and under-played,

a comparatively rare combination. Poor card-players tend to underbid, and rightly so, for their cards aren't as good as they look, not when they start playing them. Made of sterner stuff, my North was undeterred by his shortcomings.

With both sides vulnerable, West dealt and bid 1♡. North jumped to 4♠ and East came in with 5♣. What should I have done holding:

♠ K6 ♡ 5 ◇ Q1093 ♣ Q109753?

East certainly wasn't making a cue-bid on the way to a slam. Ostensibly, he was prepared to play in 5♣. Of course, he had no such intention. He expected to be doubled, and to be doubled again when he took refuge in 5♡, which he judged to be a cheap save. He knew that I knew that he was spoofing and that North wouldn't know anything anyway. The balance of confusion tilted his way.

For my part, I could only guess at North's 4♠. Pre-empting wasn't the best part of his game, nothing was, so he probably had a good hand. But how good? I couldn't tell. Maybe we had a slam — in theory, though with North at the wheel, it by no means followed that we had twelve tricks in practice.

The best result at the vulnerability would be to let opponents play in 5♣, with the expectation of collecting 800 or so. I passed and so did West. Needless to say, North doubled and East duly escaped into 5♡. My 5♠ closed the auction.

With the ♠Q coming down we made twelve tricks. In defence, on a club lead, we should have made all thirteen for a well-deserved 1100. Six clubs, always a make, would have been even more profitable, but as

S.J. Simon used to say: "Look for the best result possible, not for the best possible result." Sound advice, especially at rubber bridge.

POOR PARTNERS

Admittedly the supply of poor partners greatly exceeds the demand, yet there are times when they pay dividends which wouldn't be forthcoming from their betters. Each one, however, must be treated strictly according to his demerits as on the diagrammed hand which came up at the St James's Bridge Club. On my right was the intrepid lady we met a few pages back. She had merit, her partner had a good deal less and mine, none at all.

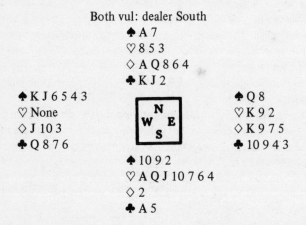

Both vul: dealer South

```
                    ♠ A 7
                    ♡ 8 5 3
                    ◇ A Q 8 6 4
                    ♣ K J 2
  ♠ K J 6 5 4 3                      ♠ Q 8
  ♡ None              N              ♡ K 9 2
  ◇ J 10 3        W       E          ◇ K 9 7 5
  ♣ Q 8 7 6          S              ♣ 10 9 4 3
                    ♠ 10 9 2
                    ♡ A Q J 10 7 6 4
                    ◇ 2
                    ♣ A 5
```

Sitting South, I dealt and opened 4♡ — the proper misbid with the partner of the moment, who would expect a strong hand from a preempt at game level. The auction took this course.

South	West	North	East
4♡	4♠	4NT	Pass
5♡	Pass	6♡	Dble
Pass	Pass	Redble	

North's 4NT wasn't so much an enquiry for aces — for he expected me to have two at least — as an expression of joy, which said: "We are going places." If there were a 39th bid to enrich the vocabulary, perhaps it should be "Whoopee!" to add to the Blackwood apparatus.

With misplaced respect for West's overcall and well-founded contempt for North's bidding, East, the intrepid lady, doubled the final contract.

When the double came round to him, West paused unhappily. Badly wanting to escape, he could find no place of refuge, and squirming, passed.

Undeterred, North redoubled. No, he wasn't hoping to drive opponents into 6♠. Far from it. He expected me to make 6♡ and it didn't occur to him that West might take it out. The squirming had been wasted on him.

Fearing to jump from the frying-pan into the fire, West passed again.

The lead was the ♠5 to dummy's ace and East's ♠8. The heart finesse at trick two revealed the not unexpected 3-0 break and it looked as if the contract would depend on my guessing in which minor to finesse so as to dispose of a spade. My third spade would then be my only loser. If I misguessed it would cost 1000. Could I do better? I looked for clues.

With spades headed by the KQ West would have led the ♠K, not the ♠5, so East was marked with a top honour, probably the ♠Q.

Since West wouldn't have bid 4♠ on a 5-card suit, a third round of trumps would be ruffed. How then could I get to dummy to repeat the trump finesse without committing myself prematurely to the right guess in the minors?

This is where it was so important for me to know that sitting over me wasn't Benito Garozzo. At trick three, after the ♠A and the trump finesse, I led the ♠10. West, wasting nothing, went up with the ♠J and East won, perforce, with the ♠Q. The intrepid lady was end-played.

A trump return, the best she could do, allowed me to repeat the finesse, and though I wasn't yet out of the wood, I could reel off my trumps, putting opponents under pressure. In the event, East discarded one diamond too many and a ruff brought down the ◇K. The club finesse being right, it didn't really matter.

This is a typical case of computing the odds at rubber bridge. The odds of guessing in which minor to finesse were 50-50. There was a better chance of a mistake by West at trick three — by this particular West. I would never have dared to adopt this line of play against a Garozzo. Quick as lightning, Benito would have gone up with the ♠K, swallowing East's ♠Q, the *Crocodile Coup*. A third spade would have allowed East to over-ruff dummy. The defence would have been obvious — to a Benito Garozzo.

Observe how many wrongs it took to make a right — the bonus of 2020 for the good guy. The singular, you will note, for North contributed to it only because he knew no better. He did his best to steer into the abyss, but lost his way.

Every bid by everyone at the table was wrong. My own play, like my opening 4♡, could be excused only by the known limitations of North and West respectively. It was a case of making the right bid with the wrong partner and the wrong play against the right opponent. All typical of rubber bridge.

A DISTORTING MIRROR

Highlighting the difference between rubber bridge and duplicate, Tannah Hirsh gives this hand which came up at the San Diego Fall Nationals in 1984.

Both vul: dealer East

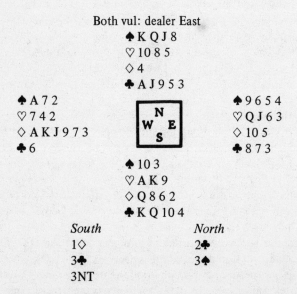

```
                ♠ K Q J 8
                ♡ 10 8 5
                ◇ 4
                ♣ A J 9 5 3
  ♠ A 7 2                        ♠ 9 6 5 4
  ♡ 7 4 2         N              ♡ Q J 6 3
  ◇ A K J 9 7 3  W   E           ◇ 10 5
  ♣ 6               S            ♣ 8 7 3
                ♠ 10 3
                ♡ A K 9
                ◇ Q 8 6 2
                ♣ K Q 10 4
```

South	North
1◇	2♣
3♣	3♠
3NT	

At rubber bridge the contract would surely be 5♣, against which there is no defence. In a pairs event minor suit games are at a heavy discount. Ten tricks in notrumps are worth more than eleven in clubs, so, since that's where most pairs will play, you do likewise.

West starts with the ◇K, ◇A and ◇J, East throwing a club on the third round. You have eight tricks. Where can you find a ninth? You daren't touch spades for West wouldn't have played as he did without an entry, which can only be the ♠A.

A double finesse in hearts offers the only hope and at rubber bridge – if you found yourself in this contract – you would take it stoically. You would go three down if it failed, but the risk would be worth taking. Not so with matchpoint scoring, for no other declarer would be likely to play that way and you would end up with a frigid bottom. Shrugging your shoulders, you take your eight tricks, concede 100 and expect something like an average.

Like a distorting mirror, matchpoint scoring deforms both the bidding and the play, and yet the premium on extra tricks has compensating attractions and often leads to brilliant play.

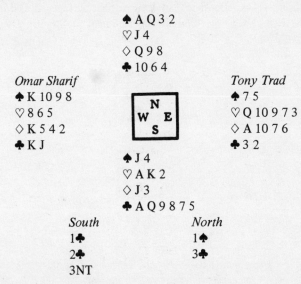

```
                    ♠ A Q 3 2
                    ♡ J 4
                    ◇ Q 9 8
                    ♣ 10 6 4
  Omar Sharif                        Tony Trad
  ♠ K 10 9 8         N               ♠ 7 5
  ♡ 8 6 5        W       E           ♡ Q 10 9 7 3
  ◇ K 5 4 2          S               ◇ A 10 7 6
  ♣ K J                              ♣ 3 2
                    ♠ J 4
                    ♡ A K 2
                    ◇ J 3
                    ♣ A Q 9 8 7 5
```

South	North
1♣	1♠
2♣	3♣
3NT	

Omar led the ◇2 to the ◇9, ◇10 and ◇J. Declarer started wtih the ♠4 to dummy's ♠Q and continued with the ♣4, finessing the ♣Q.

What's the prognosis? Defenders can take three diamonds and a club, but what else?

Omar found two more winners. On South's ♣Q, at trick three, he calmly dropped the ♣J!

Now South could see his way to scoring no fewer than eleven tricks, surely a top. The ♣J, covered by the king and ace, allowed him to run the ♣10, finessing against East's supposed ♣K. Omar pounced and cashed two spades before taking the diamonds.

Of course, seeing the ♣J, declarer could have taken his nine tricks without further ado, but the matchpoint premium on extra tricks presented an irresistible temptation — which is why Omar Sharif held it out to him.

Is this where the pairs event scores over rubber bridge? Or is there room for similar manoeuvres in the money game? It all depends on the stakes, so let's go over to New York where Ely Culbertson and Richard L. Frey are playing a rubber bridge match against France's two greatest players, Pierre Albarran and Baron Robert de Nexon. The stakes are twenty dollars a hundred, a big game today, a much bigger one in 1935 when the match was played.

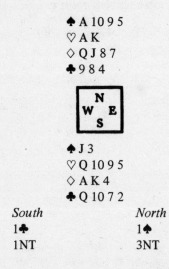

```
              ♠ A 10 9 5
              ♡ A K
              ◇ Q J 8 7
              ♣ 9 8 4

                  N
              W       E
                  S

              ♠ J 3
              ♡ Q 10 9 5
              ◇ A K 4
              ♣ Q 10 7 2
```

South	North
1♣	1♠
1NT	3NT

West leads a low spade to East's queen. A heart comes back. Declarer runs the ♣9 which wins. He now has nine certain tricks. How should he proceed?

At twenty 1935 dollars a hundred every trick was a consideration, so Richard L. Frey, who was declarer, repeated the club finesse. Robert de Nexon, East, showed out and Pierre Albarran proceeded to win the next four tricks.

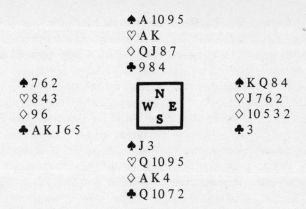

♠ A 10 9 5
♡ A K
◇ Q J 8 7
♣ 9 8 4

♠ 7 6 2
♡ 8 4 3
◇ 9 6
♣ A K J 6 5

♠ K Q 8 4
♡ J 7 6 2
◇ 10 5 3 2
♣ 3

♠ J 3
♡ Q 10 9 5
◇ A K 4
♣ Q 10 7 2

"What happened?" asked Culbertson, who liked to leave the table when partner played the hand.

"One down," replied Frey laconically.

Richard L. Frey likes to tell stories against himself. He has had too many successes to resent the successes of others, even when they are scored at his expense.

AN EASIER WAY OF LIFE

The stakes do not have to be twenty dollars a hundred, even at today's values, to give extra tricks a significance. That is why some players keep a running total of the score after every hand. In the rubber game, declarer, needing ten tricks in notrumps or eleven in a major game to win an extra point, plays accordingly, as he would in a pairs event.

There is, however, a radical difference. With matchpoint scoring the players must concentrate on every hand, for all are equally important. The part-score is worth as much as the slam. There's no let-up.

In the money game a player may relax and miss an extra trick or two without necessarily losing anything. It may not affect the rubber points at all, and if it does, no more than one point will be at stake. There's no equivalent to tops and bottoms on small hands. The result is that while there's an incentive to strive for extra tricks, the pressure isn't nearly as great. It's an easier way of life altogether.

ENTER THE KIBITZER

In the Temple of the Compleat Bridge Player there are many effigies of the kibitzer in characteristic poses, sometimes sneering, sometimes content to look knowing, always ready to give others the benefit of his unsolicited advice.

The kibitzer is not to be confused with the spectator. The latter is a rare species, if only because bridge provides so few spectacles. The former is to be found in over-abundance. Both are onlookers, but the kibitzer is a *participating onlooker*, who will tell you when the hand is over — if he can wait that long — that you should have taken a double finesse, or played for the drop, or cashed a winner you didn't have or whatever he thinks best. Since he cannot be doubled he can afford to take considerable risks.

For my part, I freely confess that I am a thoroughly incompetent kibitzer, with no interest in other people's misfortunes, except when I am waiting to cut in. Then I am wholeheartedly on declarer's side and I resent it if he misplays the hand, for it means that I shall be kept waiting, instead of keeping others waiting. This is the sort of thing I find hard to forgive.

Both vul: dealer South

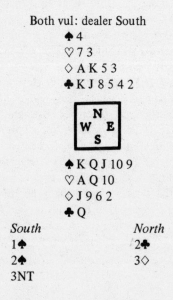

```
          ♠ 4
          ♡ 7 3
          ◇ A K 5 3
          ♣ K J 8 5 4 2

              N
           W     E
              S

          ♠ K Q J 10 9
          ♡ A Q 10
          ◇ J 9 6 2
          ♣ Q
```

South	*North*
1♠	2♣
2♠	3◇
3NT	

West led the ♡6 to East's ♡J and South's ♡Q. I looked at my watch. I had time for one quick rubber if South made his contract. If he went down I could wait no longer.

The danger was obvious. If East gained the lead before declarer had time to develop nine tricks, a heart through the closed hand could be fatal. Which black suit, then, should he tackle first?

The answer seemed so obvious that I couldn't imagine what South was thinking about. I learned afterwards that he was working out the odds. A 3-3 club break, one chance in three, would solve the problem, while clearing the spades would still leave him a trick short. Against that was the chance of finding a doubleton ♢Q, or alternatively, of end-playing West if he had ♢Qxx. Apparently, all this added up to more than the chances of a 3-3 club break, plus finding a doubleton ♣109.

After prolonged thought, South led a spade and finding West with the ace made game and the table was up. But for his thoroughly undeserved good luck I would have been robbed of my last rubber.

Not being a mathematician I have no idea whether or not declarer's calculations were correct, but this I do know — they were altogether irrelevant. The odds against a 3-3 club break didn't come into it.

How would South have played had he had the ♣2 instead of the ♢2? Crossing to dummy in diamonds, he would have led a low club. If East went up with the ♣A he would have had nine tricks. If he didn't, or if West had it, there would be time to set up the spades. And that's how South should have played now. Not knowing that the ♣Q was bare no sane East would have gone up with the ♣A.

I felt much more indulgent in a similar situation when this hand came up:

N/S vul: dealer West

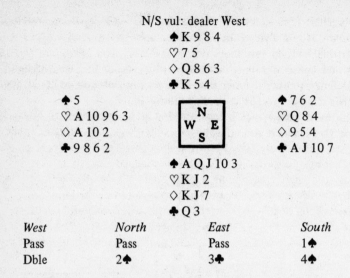

♠ K 9 8 4
♡ 7 5
◇ Q 8 6 3
♣ K 5 4

♠ 5
♡ A 10 9 6 3
◇ A 10 2
♣ 9 8 6 2

♠ 7 6 2
♡ Q 8 4
◇ 9 5 4
♣ A J 10 7

♠ A Q J 10 3
♡ K J 2
◇ K J 7
♣ Q 3

West	North	East	South
Pass	Pass	Pass	1♠
Dble	2♠	3♣	4♠

West, a player of international standing, led the ♣2 to the ♣10 and
♣Q. Declarer took three rounds of trumps, ending in dummy, and
continued with the ◇3 to his ◇J. West won and persisted with clubs,
but declarer was now in full command. He ruffed a third club, cashed
three diamonds, throwing a heart, and took the finesse against the ♡Q.
West, being marked wtih the ♡A on his double, South couldn't go
wrong. The rubber was up and all was well.

I could see no flaw in the bidding, the play or the defence, but
waiting with me was Martin Hoffman, Britain's most successful pairs
player and a brilliant kibitzer.

"What a feeble defence!" he said to me while the players were
agreeing the score. "Fancy going up with the ◇A. If he plays low and
South goes on with the ◇K, East ducks again. He wins the third time
and a club through dummy, followed by another, leaves declarer with
one trump. He can't use it to cross to dummy, since there's still a club
out, so he must lead hearts from hand."

A disturbing thought. Had East played low I should have still been
sitting out.

"Mind you," went on Martin, while the players were trying to trace
a missing 100, "that ◇J was ridiculous. Whom was he kidding? If he
plays the ◇K there's no defence. Should East hold off, declarer plays
another diamond, winning in dummy unless East rises with the ace.
Either way he has an entry to lead hearts from the table. Of course,"

concluded Hoffman, "South should have played a heart when he was in dummy after drawing trumps. A silly play, that diamond . . . "

Martin Hoffman gets more out of the game than others do, for he finds and solves not only his own problems, but those of declarers and defenders alike, at other tables. He is genuinely interested in other people's affairs. A truly outstanding kibitzer.

The hand below was one of Hoffman's selections for *Defence in Depth*. He showed it around while he was still writing the book.

Both vul: dealer East
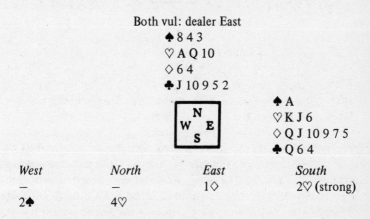

♠ 8 4 3
♡ A Q 10
♢ 6 4
♣ J 10 9 5 2

♠ A
♡ K J 6
♢ Q J 10 9 7 5
♣ Q 6 4

West	North	East	South
–	–	1♢	2♡ (strong)
2♠	4♡		

West leads the ♠K. What do you return and how do you see the future?

Your first reaction on seeing dummy will be one of surprise, no doubt, that South could find a jump overcall, advertised as "strong", on a suit headed by the nine. Evidently his requirements for a strong overcall are not very exacting, but even so he must surely have the AKs in both minors. What's his shape? With a 7-card suit West might have ventured into something better than 2♠, a pre-emptive 4♠, perhaps. With only five and not a rag outside he could have hardly found a bid at all. Almost certainly he has six spades. Step by step, you can form a pretty accurate picture of South's hand. The full deal must be, as indeed it was:

♠ 8 4 3
♡ A Q 10
◇ 6 4
♣ J 10 9 5 2

♠ K Q 10 9 7 6   ♠ A
♡ 2   ♡ K J 6
◇ 8 3 2   ◇ Q J 10 9 7 5
♣ 8 7 3   ♣ Q 6 4

♠ J 5 2
♡ 9 8 7 5 4 3
◇ A K
♣ A K

Sitting East, can you defeat the contract? Your natural play at trick two is a diamond, but see what will happen. Declarer will cash his AKs and duck a trump into your hand. Your best return, or rather the least lethal, will be another diamond. South will throw a spade, ruff in dummy and lead a club, picking up your ♣Q. Next he will cross to the ♡A and throw his other spade on the ♣J. You will ruff, scoring your third trick, but it will be your last.

Is the contract unbeatable then? Not at trick two. After the ♠A, try returning the ♡6, right into the jaws of dummy's tenace. It will cost a trick, but it will be worth two, for it will remove a vital entry from dummy. Declarer will still be able to set up the clubs by cashing the ♣AK, crossing to the ♡A and ruffing the ♣Q, but there will no longer be a way back to dummy, for you will be sitting with the ♡K over dummy's ♡Q. Instead of losing two trumps and one spade, declarer will lose one trump trick only, but three spades.

When the hand came up in a match, East didn't find the killing defence and so the contract was duly made.

"Were you East or were you on the other side?" I asked Martin.

"No, no, I wasn't playing. It was just a board I happened to kibitz."

Martin Hoffman brings off many fine plays at rubber bridge and at duplicate — not least when he is kibitzing.

It is because I am so poor a kibitzer myself, never knowing what's going on when my interests are not involved, that in so many examples in this chapter I have myself played a part, not always, I fear, crowned with glory. By and large, my partners have been poor, and one or other of my opponents, little better. The composition of the table, the balance of weakness, dictated the tactics. It's my turn to have a good partner, so to conclude I present a curious hand I had with Martin Hoffman — whom the reader has just met as a sparkling kibitzer.

THE LEMMINGS COUP

Hoffman deals the first hand of the rubber and bids 1NT (12-14). His left-hand opponent calls 2♠. What should I say, holding:

♠ Q ♡ Q643 ◇ Q752 ♣ AK53 ?

Had my partner been the intrepid lady we met earlier I would have bid 3NT. A raise to 2NT would have made the worst of both worlds for she would have bid 3NT automatically and after such a sequence we could have been doubled. A direct raise to game is rarely doubled.

With the kamikazi partner, who redoubled 6♡, only a pass could ensure safety.

Having Martin Hoffman opposite, I doubled. While game for our side was, at best, speculative, I could rely on an effective defence and therefore on a penalty of some kind. In a pairs event the decision might have been close. At rubber bridge 'money in the bank' is always a sound policy. This is what happened.

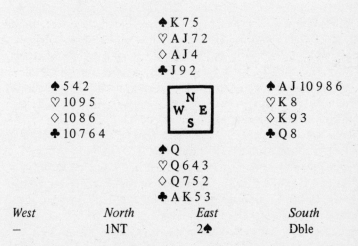

<pre>
                    ♠ K 7 5
                    ♡ A J 7 2
                    ◇ A J 4
                    ♣ J 9 2
  ♠ 5 4 2   ┌─────┐   ♠ A J 10 9 8 6
  ♡ 10 9 5   │ N │   ♡ K 8
  ◇ 10 8 6   W │   │ E   ◇ K 9 3
  ♣ 10 7 6 4   │ S │   ♣ Q 8
                    └─────┘
                    ♠ Q
                    ♡ Q 6 4 3
                    ◇ Q 7 5 2
                    ♣ A K 5 3
</pre>

West	North	East	South
—	1NT	2♠	Dble

I started with the two top clubs, then, leaving clubs alone, for a safe exit later, I switched to the ♠Q.

Pity declarer's plight. Already, at trick three, he was suffering all the pangs of an end-play. If he ducked, he would lose a second trump trick. So he won. If he played a red card, it would cost a trick, so perforce he led a spade. Hoffman won and returned another spade. With the sword of Damocles grazing his neck, declarer had to play away from one of his kings. A diamond seemed best, but now that third club proved lethal, for once more declarer had no choice. If he bared one of his kings, we would persist with the suit forcing him to bare the other or to ruff. So he ruffed the ♣J, but that, of course, only delayed the inevitable. His fate was sealed. He scored five trump tricks and no more.

I still don't know what to call this curious play. A progressive end-play? A squeeze without a squeeze card? It has the elements of both, but qualifies for neither. Perhaps the *Lemmings Coup* best describes it, an inexorable destiny compelling declarer to commit suicide, trick by trick.

CHAPTER EIGHT

The Hall of Eternal Life

Meteors flash through the skies, comets with incandescent tails leave liquid fire in their wake. We are dazzled, awestruck. But the spectacle doesn't last and, as the lights fade, the darkness closes in again.

And so it is in the world of bridge. Great players have displayed their brilliant gifts before us. Schenken, Meredith and Helen Sobel have shone and sparkled and passed away. Others remain and their exploits will surely be recalled. But which of them will 'leave their footprints in the sands of time'?

On a mound rising beside the Temple of the Compleat Bridge Player stands a small pavilion with Corinthian columns, built in the style of ancient Greece. Inside a lofty chamber, taking its name from the lake beside it, is the Hall of Eternal Life. It houses the statues of five men and one woman, who have made history, not only in bridge, but through bridge in the world beyond it. They will live when names that are household words today have receded into the distant past. Each one of them can say: *Non omnis moriar multaque pars mihi vitabit.** . . . (Horace)

CULBERTSON THE LAW GIVER

Presiding at the entrance to the Hall is the statue erected to Ely Culbertson the Law Giver. The Solon of bridge, he laid down the structure of bidding, which in its essentials survives to this day. Within a few years millions throughout the world, switching from Auction to Contract, learned to speak the same language, to use the same measures, to apply the same standards. Ely brought order out of chaos, and a game which had been the preserve of the well-to-do and the professional classes, soon spread like wildfire, quickly engulfing the huge, amorphous

---

* Not all of me will die. A great part will live on. . . .

middle classes. For this transformation Ely Culbertson was largely responsible. Ambitious, dynamic, ruthless, a superb showman, he knew how to make his dreams come true, to goad his rivals into set-piece battles and to annihilate them in a blaze of ballyhoo worthy of a Presidential Election.

The extravaganza of the Battle of the Century match, which established Culbertson's supremacy and brought him fame and fortune, has never been equalled and will surely never be surpassed. It made bigger headlines and claimed more space in the press, more time on the radio, than any event in baseball, boxing or football. From three specially set-up telegraph rooms in New York's Chatham Hotel, where the first half of the match was played, 85,000 words went out daily, describing the battle card by card — and insult by insult.

Turning bad manners into an art, Ely set out to exasperate Sidney Lenz, standard bearer of the Official System, and so his principal opponent, by ploys which it would be charitable to describe as gamesmanship.

Arriving late for every session, he regularly took his meals at the card table. Lenz complained that he was getting grease all over the cards. "Why don't you eat at the proper time like the rest of us?" he asked irritably.

"My public won't let me," replied Ely coyly.

Knowing that Lenz liked the game to move fast, Culbertson paused at every opportunity. If none presented itself, he conjured one up. Some of his trances seemed interminable. As a counter Lenz would ostentatiously pick up a book. On one occasion he exploded: "I'm going to a speakeasy to get a drink." He did.

"I play men, not cards," Ely told a reporter who questioned his tactics.

As at the card table, so in the world at large, psychology was Culbertson's favourite weapon. He boasted of the sexual connotation he had devised for his system — 'approach', 'forcing', 'one over one'. He made a special appeal to women — who had more time for the game than men — by projecting the idea that proficiency at bridge, in other words mastery of his system, would enable them to assert superiority over less well instructed males.

It is usually accepted that as a player Culbertson was as good as the best in his day. But was he any better? It's doubtful. What is certain is that his psychological gifts brought him many points, especially at rubber bridge. There were times, we are told by Richard L. Frey, one of his associates, when the wages of the hard-pressed staff at the *Bridge World*, which he founded, came out of his winnings.

This hand, which would deserve a place of honour in the chapter on *The Sixth and other Senses*, came up in the 99th rubber of the Battle of the Century.

Love all: dealer West

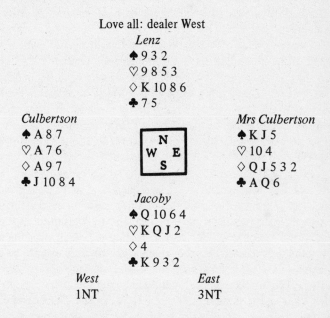

Lenz
♠ 9 3 2
♡ 9 8 5 3
◇ K 10 8 6
♣ 7 5

Culbertson
♠ A 8 7
♡ A 7 6
◇ A 9 7
♣ J 10 8 4

Mrs Culbertson
♠ K J 5
♡ 10 4
◇ Q J 5 3 2
♣ A Q 6

Jacoby
♠ Q 10 6 4
♡ K Q J 2
◇ 4
♣ K 9 3 2

West	East
1NT	3NT

Note the weak notrump, more than ever popular in Britain, but no longer favoured by most of the experts in America.

Lenz led the ◇6, a lucky start for declarer. Winning with the ◇9, Culbertson went on with the suit, setting up two diamonds in dummy. Jacoby, South, discarded the ♣2 and the ♠4. In with the ◇K, Lenz switched to a heart, Ely holding up his ace till the third round.

He could see eight tricks. Where should he look for the ninth – the spade or the club finesse, or was there, perhaps, a better way?

Culbertson began by cashing the ♣A, the key move. Next came the ◇QJ. Coming down to four cards, Oswald Jacoby was inexorably squeezed. If he parted with his fourth heart, he would be thrown in with the ♣K and forced to lead into the spade tenace. So he threw a spade, allowing Culbertson to pick up his queen.

Why should Ely play this way in preference to taking a simple finesse? His explanation is instructive and in keeping with his dictum, "I play the man, not the cards."

Having scored two tricks in hearts, says Culbertson, Jacoby sat back, visibly relaxed. Evidently he thought he could defeat the contract. Why? Presumably because he had both the ♠Q and the ♣K. "I played accordingly," concludes Ely.

To execute the combination squeeze-end-play called for sound technique. To conceive it required something more — psychology and an acute perception of the vibrations around him. Both these gifts Culbertson exhibited to a remarkable degree in launching Contract upon a society, which, it seems, had been waiting for it impatiently.

Ely's flamboyance, his arrogance, his provocative, often offensive remarks are recalled from time to time. "He made a mint by putting his worst foot forward," says Jack Olsen in *The Mad World of Bridge*.

His great achievements, equalled by none, have all but passed into oblivion.

> *The evil that men do lives after them*
> *The good is 'oft forgot and interred with their bones.*

CHARLES GOREN: A MAN OR A MYTH?

From Culbertson's statue, with its surrealist touches, we pass on to that of his successor, Charles Goren. No greater challenge could have faced the sculptor, for Goren, long ago, became an institution and is today more of a legend than a mere man. How can the clay be moulded to portray a legend?

If the cornerstone of Culbertson's success was the Approach Forcing System, Goren's was an adaptation which became known as Standard American. Each, in turn, mesmerised the American public and gained recognition in distant parts of the world.

Goren's distinctive contribution was the substitution of the Milton Work Points Count — the 4-3-2-1 scale for aces, kings, queens and knaves — for honour tricks. Ignored in its native America, the Points Count was used by all the leading players in England long before the war. Goren rediscovered it in 1949.* By then he was the premier player, teacher and writer in the States, widely known as 'Mr Bridge'. His authority was unquestioned, and soon the Point Count became the national currency.

For eighteen years, from 1944 to 1962, Charles Goren headed the Master Points Winners list. He sold more books, gave more lectures and

---

* The author's *Streamlined Bridge*, based entirely on the Point Count, was published in England in 1947.

made more money than Culbertson in all his glory. But unlike Ely, who traded on his abrasive, provocative style, capitalising on his ill manners, Goren was essentially the 'nice guy', correct, considerate, chivalrous. A shining example to others, Goren was as anxious to be St George as Culbertson was to be the Dragon. Never before or since the reign of "Mr Bridge" has the game enjoyed so favourable a public image.

What was Goren like as a player? His soured rivals often spoke of him disparagingly, ascribing his success to hard work and the talents of his partner, Helen Sobel. Rivals are rarely the best judges. I only saw Charles Goren in action once, at Selfridges in London, but his plays have been recorded and they leave no room for doubt that in his day he was right at the top. I will give two examples. The first deal came up in the American Life Master Pairs in 1958.

Both vul: dealer South

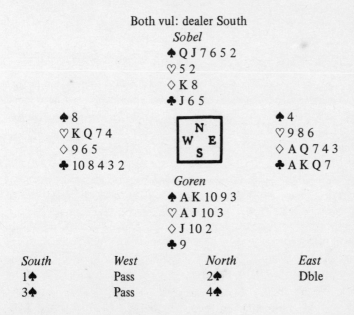

Sobel
♠ Q J 7 6 5 2
♡ 5 2
◇ K 8
♣ J 6 5

♠ 8
♡ K Q 7 4
◇ 9 6 5
♣ 10 8 4 3 2

♠ 4
♡ 9 8 6
◇ A Q 7 4 3
♣ A K Q 7

Goren
♠ A K 10 9 3
♡ A J 10 3
◇ J 10 2
♣ 9

South	West	North	East
1♠	Pass	2♠	Dble
3♠	Pass	4♠	

West led the ♡K, East following with the ♡6. Since E/W could certainly make 4♣, even one down would ensure a good result, but making the contract would surely be a top or thereabouts. Could it be done?

After the lead of the ♡K, indicating the Q, declarer should assume that every other card would be wrong, as in the diagram. How, then, can he avoid losing a heart, two diamonds and a club?

Goren found a way of avoiding the unavoidable. Winning the first trick with the ♡A, he laid down the ♠A and continued with the ♡3. West played the ♡7 but, as Goren had hoped, East couldn't help overtaking with the ♡8, and now the contract was safe. The ♡J forced the ♡Q, whereupon the ♡10 took care of one of dummy's diamond losers.

The hand below, from a teams event, belongs to an earlier vintage.

```
                    ♠ Q 10 4
                    ♡ 7 4 2
                    ◇ J 7 3 2
                    ♣ K Q 8
  ♠ J 8 7 6 5                          ♠ 9 3
  ♡ J              ┌──────────┐        ♡ 10 5 3
  ◇ 8             │    N     │         ◇ Q 10 9 4
  ♣ A 10 9 7 3 2  │  W   E   │         ♣ J 6 5 4
                  │    S     │
                  └──────────┘
                    ♠ A K 2
                    ♡ A K Q 9 8 6
                    ◇ A K 6 5
                    ♣ None
```

West led the ♡J against Goren's 6♡. After drawing trumps, Goren continued with the two top diamonds. When West showed out, the contract appeared to be doomed. With Nemesis hot on his heels, how did Charles Goren continue to trip her up? Even seeing all four hands, the solution isn't easy to find.

To compensate for the unlucky diamond break, Goren had to find two cards well placed. First he cashed the ♠A, then he finessed the ♠10. Next he led the ♣K, jettisoning his ♠K. Whichever black card West returned, and he had no others, dummy's two queens would take care of the losing diamonds.

Only a very fine player could have made the contract.

Goren's team won the Vanderbilt in 1962. That was his last success in a major event and by then he was already past his prime. His health, and with it his formidable energy, were waning. No longer could he say, as he had done once: "I never work more than twenty-four hours a day." The spirit was willing, but the flesh was no longer up to it.

Yet never has the name of Goren enjoyed such prominence, as after he had left the bridge scene. Teams bearing his name contested and won major events. Articles with the Goren by-line, books, prefaces, endorsements, cascaded from the Goren headquarters in New York. *Travel with Goren* remains to this day the biggest commercial undertaking of its kind in the world. No one has travelled with Goren for many years. No one expects to do so now, but holidays, and more especially cruises, with the Goren cachet attract a constant stream of bridge players.

Harold Ogust was, for years, the moving spirit of *Travel with Goren*. Tannah Hirsch is his successor. For decades the written word owed just about everything to Richard L. Frey, America's top publicist since the days of Culbertson. On both sides of the Atlantic there have been ghosts, and ghosts ghosting for ghosts. But the authority, the quality of the Goren output has never been challenged. Under the Goren colours every horse from the stables was a thoroughbred.

Charles Goren retired to Florida, then to California, long, long ago, but the legend lives on and will never die. His place in the Hall of Eternal Life is assured.

PERROUX: THE EXORCIST

A few short steps but a vast distance separate the monuments to Culbertson and Goren from that erected to Carlo Alberto Perroux, founder and leader of Italy's invincible *squadra azzurra*.

The Americans measured success in terms of money. Perroux despised money. Rarely are Culbertson or Goren mentioned without some reference to their huge incomes, their vast fortunes, the fabulous fees they commanded for personal appearances. Perroux never made a penny out of bridge, and so long as he was in command, neither did any member of the Blue Team. He recalls with a wistful smile the only gift he ever made to one of 'his boys', a doll to the daughter of Giorgio Belladonna on her fifth birthday. They were in New York at the time and the doll, 'made in Japan', cost him one dollar-fifty.

When the American influence and the lure of commercialism proved too strong to resist, Perroux chose to retire. He had no wish to lead a team of 'acrobats performing in a circus'. His 'boys' had always been amateurs, and amateurs they would remain so long as he was there. On that there could be no compromise.

With the departure of Carlo Alberto Perroux the era of the amateurs in bridge came to an end. Is that, I wonder, such a good thing?

For Culbertson and Goren success was a personal matter, their partners and their teams being incidental to their individual triumphs. The ego, unleashed, reigned supreme, naked and unashamed with Ely Culbertson, decorously and discreetly draped in the case of Charles Goren.

The opposite applies to Perroux, and therein lies his greatest achievement. He subjugated the ego, proving once and for all that the immovable object can stop the irresistible force. Imbued with the team spirit, the most talented players in the world subordinated their individual personalities to the common good, and so won victory after victory.

"How is it that you always won?" I asked Perroux, shortly after he had retired. "Are the Italians really so much better than anyone else?"

"By no means," he replied. "The British, the French and the Americans have players of the same calibre, but they lack the *spirito de squadra*, and that is decisive."

The jealousies, the rivalries, the tantrums, the temperamental outbursts which lowered, and sometimes ruined the performance of other contenders were unknown to the Italians.

Edgar Kaplan records the incredulous exclamation of an American spectator after one of the Blue Team's victories: "Why, they positively like each other."

I cannot recall such a remark, except in jest, being made about any other team.

In listing the qualities required to reach the top in international bridge Perroux puts team spirit first and foremost. So does Giorgio Belladonna, whose order of priorities is: team spirit, psychology, ability. In *Dentro Bridge Con Belladonna* (vol. 2) he explains: 'I must emphasise that some players, renowned for their talents at bridge, often have a disastrous effect on a team's results, while others, less gifted technically, may raise the overall performance.' The former sometimes strikes a harsh, discordant note; the latter can make for harmony.

"A hundred of the world's most gifted musicians wouldn't make an orchestra," was one of Perroux's remarks. "They would need a conductor to weld them into one."

As the conductor of the Blue Team, Perroux had an advantage not enjoyed by anyone in Britain, America or France. With the title 'Technical Director' he was, in fact, a dictator, who picked his team unsaddled by the democratic processes imposed on selectors elsewhere. A benign but ruthless disciplinarian, he ordained from Modena that every other week Forquet should go to Rome or Garozzo visit Naples to practise together. Every weekend Pabis-Ticci was called upon to travel from Florence to Rome to play with D'Alelio and to give a good game to Avarelli and Belladonna.

If the battle of Waterloo was won on the playing fields of Eton, the fate of the Bermuda Bowl must have been decided in the study of Carlo Alberto Perroux in Modena.

During international events many players see a chance to combine pleasure with pleasure, to play bridge by day and to enjoy the odd peccadillo by night. No such licence was ever extended to the Blue Team. They were expected to resist temptation. Sometimes this posed problems, as at the European Championships in Vienna in 1957.

An early riser, Perroux was surprised one day to see Belladonna walk into the Grand Hotel at dawn. Of course, says Perroux, he might have spent the night praying at the tomb of the Hapsburgs. Perroux wouldn't speculate, but it was an irrevocable rule that members of the *squadra azzurra* should sleep at night. So, to make sure, he placed Roberto Bianchi, who had accompanied the team to Vienna, as a 'watchdog' in Belladonna's double room. All went well for forty-eight hours. Then, on his early rounds, Perroux gently opened the door and found both beds empty.

The situation called for extreme measures. When play ended that night he accompanied Giorgio to his room and removed all his trousers — "tutti i pantaloni". Thereafter there were no more escapades.

The story of Forquet's honeymoon is another example of the merciless discipline imposed on the *squadra azzurra*.

Pietro Forquet was married to Guiliana on the eve of the 1964 Olympiad, so they spent their honeymoon during the hurly-burly of a great international bridge contest. All went well, matrimonially speaking, until the arrival of Carlo Alberto Perroux. The day after he reached the scene the Italians were due to meet the British who were leading the field. With so gruelling a test before them, Perroux decided that ardent bridegroom and radiant bride should be separated for the night. So he sent Pabis-Ticci to Pietro's room and Guiliana to Signora Pabis-Ticci's. Italy's next encounter was to be against the tough Americans, and again Perroux laid it down that the honeymoon couple should not spend the night together.

Having heard Perroux's views on the paramount importance of the *spirito de squadra*, I asked him what gifts were required of a great captain. His order was: authority, prestige, psychology and patience. But, if the members have a genuine affection for their captain, there is less need for authority and prestige. "It was always enough to ask, I didn't have to command," he told me.

The team spirit, discipline, constant practice, natural ability, all played a part in ensuring year after year the *squadra azzurra*'s unquestioned superiority. But there was more to it than that, said Perroux, looking back on some of the happiest days of his life. "There was a certain mysticism. We really felt that we were doing something important for our country."

Dulce est pro patria mori — and sweeter still to live and win.

The mystical touch was in keeping with Perroux's mission. He cast a spell in which the team spirit was the most potent incantation. Yet it was only the means to an end, which was to exorcise the evil spirits that plague us all, but none so much as gifted bridge players. The ultimate goal was to subdue the rampant ego, the 'enemy within' and it is as the Great Exorcist that Carlo Alberto Perroux will be justly remembered.

IRA CORN: A SALIENT INTO THE FUTURE

Close to Perroux's stands the massive statue to Ira Corn, self-made Texan multi-millionaire, who saw in bridge the answer to the problems posed by leisure in the modern affluent society. Millions played bridge, yet many millions more didn't. To bring within the reach of all the most fascinating, stimulating game in the world was Ira Corn's grand design, and the first step in its execution was to regain for America the Bermuda Bowl, the sceptre of world bridge supremacy.

For fifteen lean years the Americans had been suffering the painful withdrawal symptoms of compulsive winners. Their last success was in 1954 in Monte Carlo. England won in 1955, the French the year after. Then came an uninterrupted series of victories for Italy.

Watching the *squadra azzurra* carry all before them in the New York Olympiad in 1964, Ira Corn asked himself: what is the secret of their success?

And he came up with the answer. They are a team, a closely integrated unit, and all we have to put against them are gifted individuals, pairs at best, formed one day, dissolved the next.

"What has she got that I haven't?" asked a girl piqued by her boyfriend's interest in the latest sex symbol.

"Nothing, nothing at all," was the reply. "It's just that she groups it better."

The Italians grouped it better, much better.

Again Corn posed the question: Why?

Geography provided one of the answers. Perroux could bring his best players together and keep them in constant practice without calling on anyone to travel more than some 200 miles, from Rome to Naples. More than 4500 miles lie between New York and Los Angeles.

Corn set out to put that right. Pitting dollars against distance, he picked six of America's most promising young players and brought them together to live within easy reach of his house in Dallas. All were professionals, dedicated to bridge. Single men were paid 10,000 dollars a year, married men 15,000 dollars. With allowances and generous bonuses on top, they were relieved of all financial worries and could devote their whole time, their energies and their thoughts, to the supreme goal — the return of the Bermuda Bowl across the Atlantic.

Joe Musumeci, 'Moose' for short, a retired Air Force officer, was appointed trainer, disciplinarian and deputy captain. To keep fit the Aces went jogging. To keep in tune with each other, when temperamental difficulties arose, they had the services of a psychiatrist. They were provided with an office, a secretary, huge filing cabinets and a terminal linked to the Computer Centre in Houston — of which Ira Corn was a director.

On a visit to Dallas, Bobby Goldman invited me to test it. "Let's have something typically British," he suggested. I chose Acol Two Bids and within minutes he was reeling off reams of tape with dozens of hands tailored to my specifications, facing random dummies. Through an inter-office communications instrument, known as 'the squawk box', I bid the hands with Bobby Wolff, then with Jim Jacoby, every bidding sequence and every contract being subjected to critical analysis by the other Aces.

With a profusion of examples, available at a moment's notice, the Aces could test their methods, in attack and in defence in situations which would not come up often enough at the table to allow adequate practice.

In Ira Corn's house at 4829 Forest Lane, a few minutes' drive from their offices, the Aces were always at home. Like their husbands, the wives, all Life Masters, were as ardent in pursuit of the Bermuda Bowl as the knights of old in their quest for the Holy Grail. The future of one and all depended on it.

Betsy Wolff was the *châtelaine*. Dorothy Moore, for many years Ira's close friend, was the Queen Mother, alive to all the vibrations, anticipating every ripple that could cause friction. Dorothy knew exactly what she wanted — and what everyone else should want. And she would let one and all have their way — so long as it coincided with hers. "No problem" was her motto. Everyone liked her, and above all, trusted her.

If Perroux could be proud of *il spirito de squadra*, Ira and Dorothy could be no less proud of *il spirito de famiglia*.

As I chatted to the Aces and looked across the room at their trophies, lined up on the mantelpiece, I couldn't help thinking of the ditty which begins: *As I was walking up the stair I met a man who wasn't there.* That man was Carlo Alberto Perroux. Ira Corn, who had never met him, seemed to be saying: "Anything you can do, I can do better."

To keep the Aces in constant practice Ira Corn invited the strongest teams in America to be his guests in Dallas. From the East Coast and the West Coast, from Canada and from Mexico, the best players came to Forest Lane, stayed in Ira's spacious mansion and engaged the Aces in long, gruelling matches.

When the Aces attended the big national tournaments to compete for the major trophies, the Spingold and the Vanderbilt, they presented a spectacle never seen before — or since. All wore the same attire, laid down in directives by Moose for every event.

Saturday: Red and gold
Sunday: Grey and blue
Monday: Blue and blue, polka dot ties . . .

In their distinctive uniforms — "the most polite and gentlemanly players I have ever seen", as Alan Sobel, America's leading tournament director, described them — the Aces were truly a *corps d'élite*.

Early in 1970 the Aces met Omar Sharif's Circus in the longest match of all time, 840 boards played over two months in seven of America's biggest cities. With Benito Garozzo, Giorgio Belladonna and, in the closing stages, Pietro Forquet, the bluest of the Blues, the Circus was, in all but name, the *squadra azzurra* itself. When, on Sunday 1 March, the cards were replaced in their slots on the last board of the match, the Aces had defeated the Circus by 101 IMPs.

To quote Billy Eisenberg: "That night in Philadelphia we knew that we had arrived."

The moment of truth was to come three months later — at the World Championship in Stockholm. Alas, what was to have been a gripping, first-class drama quickly turned into a vapid, second-class comedy. The Blue Team, holders of the world title since 1956, withdrew, leaving a team of 'tourists', as a critic described them, to carry Italy's colours. Taiwan, having beaten America to take second place in Rio de Janeiro the year before, provided the main opposition.

The Aces carried all before them. It was no fault of theirs if their opponents were unworthy of their mettle. The following year, in Taipeh, they defended their title successfully against a much stronger field which included the French, starring Jaïs and Trézel, winners of the European Championship, and America's official team. The Aces were playing as the holders of the world title. That they happened to be Americans was incidental.

Having conceived the Aces, nursed them, trained them, and spent a fortune in bringing them to the threshold of victory, Ira withdrew discreetly to watch its consummation from the sidelines. Before the footlights, leading the Aces into battle as their captain in Taipeh, as in Stockholm the year before, was Oswald Jacoby. Ira's modest role was to open the champagne at the celebrations. With a radiant smile he toasted the team and their captain.

Humility is an unusual trait in self-made millionaires, but then Ira Corn was, in every sense, a very unusual man. Standing 6 foot 3 inches tall, weighing 300 lbs, everything about him seemed larger than life — his dynamic drive, his iron will, his vision, sweeping beyond the horizons into the distant future.

In America, where bridge professionalism is so much more widespread and more highly developed than anywhere else, rich sponsors are not unknown. Several have been rich enough and good enough, with the aid of their betters, to reach the top. But one and all insisted on playing themselves. Having paid the pipers, they were not content to call the tunes. They wanted to strike some of the notes, too. A very human failing, no doubt, but not one that afflicted Ira Corn. Neither vanity nor conceit had any part in his make-up. The first, vital part of his dream had come true. He had brought the Bermuda Bowl back to America. That was substance. He didn't insist on basking in the shadow.

Unlike other rich sponsors, he had never picked himself to play for his team. Even in practice matches he came in only if one of the Aces fell out at the last moment. This was certainly not due to lack of technical ability, but as the Executive Director of the fastest-growing conglomerate in Texas he had too many other interests to dedicate himself to the game in the manner he expected of his Janissaries.

In 1963, with Dorothy Moore, he had won the National Mixed Pairs Championship. By any standard he was a class player.

Any expert could be proud of the defence he found on the hand overleaf, which came up in a practice match.

The reader may have seen the deal before, notably in *The Other Side of Bridge*, but it is only fitting to recall it here, for it has a cachet which other rich sponsors would find it hard to match.

E/W vul: dealer East

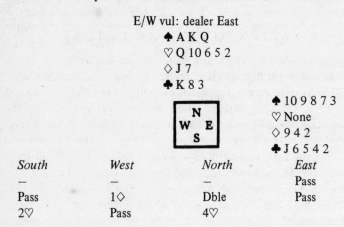

♠ A K Q
♡ Q 10 6 5 2
◇ J 7
♣ K 8 3

♠ 10 9 8 7 3
♡ None
◇ 9 4 2
♣ J 6 5 4 2

South	West	North	East
—	—	—	Pass
Pass	1◇	Dble	Pass
2♡	Pass	4♡	

Bobby Wolff, sitting West, led the ◇K. How would you see the future from Ira's position as East?

You would expect two tricks in diamonds and either a trick in trumps or in clubs, but surely not both. The only feeble ray of hope was that void in trumps, for there was nothing to tell declarer that the suit would break so badly. That gave Ira an idea. He would signal a doubleton diamond and maybe the threat of a ruff would promote a trick for Bobby Wolff. To the ◇K he followed with the ◇9. On the ◇A he echoed with the ◇2. Bobby duly led a third diamond and declarer, thinking that he could well afford it, ruffed with dummy's ♡10.

This was the full deal:

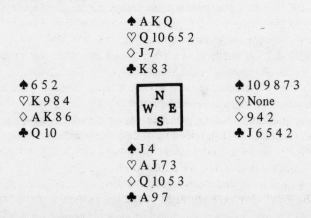

♠ A K Q
♡ Q 10 6 5 2
◇ J 7
♣ K 8 3

♠ 6 5 2
♡ K 9 8 4
◇ A K 8 6
♣ Q 10

♠ 10 9 8 7 3
♡ None
◇ 9 4 2
♣ J 6 5 4 2

♠ J 4
♡ A J 7 3
◇ Q 10 5 3
♣ A 9 7

Now Bobby had two certain trump tricks. Ira Corn had contrived a trump promotion with a void!

A SALIENT INTO THE FUTURE

Victory, symbolised by the return of the Bermuda Bowl, pride in the Aces and confidence in the future, revived America's interest in bridge. In 1970 the press gave more space to bridge news than during the whole of the preceding fifteen years. Before 1971 had reached the half-way stage the 1970 figures had been left far behind. The second part of Corn's grand design was beginning to unfold. He had driven a salient into the future and bridge was about to take its rightful place in public life. One major obstacle still stood in the way. The doors to television coverage remained closed, and unlike Culbertson, or even Goren, the Aces had no one, least of all Ira Corn himself, to inspire a personality cult.

Television called for glamour. Who could provide it?

The sculptor has caught the smile on Ira's features as he looks invitingly to the statue beside him. Omar Sharif returns the smile.

OMAR SHARIF BLAZES A TRAIL

Born out of his time, Omar Sharif would have felt thoroughly at home in Renaissance Florence. Like Lorenzo the Magnificent, he was pre-destined to be a patron of the arts. Lorenzo was a poet. Omar's art is bridge and he is more passionately devoted to it than was any Medici to poetry or painting.

Where Ira Corn saw in bridge an answer to the problems posed by leisure in the affluent society, Omar Sharif believed that it would raise the quality of life and improve human relations.

"What do you think of the news from Cairo?" he was once asked when a crisis threatened in the Middle East.

"If they played bridge they wouldn't have so much time to hate each other," was the characteristic reply.

Omar practised what he preached. As captain of the Egyptian team, he was forced more than once to withdraw from matches against Israel. To demonstrate his true feelings he invited the Israelis to games in private and made sure that the public knew about it.

How could the under-privileged, the disadvantaged, the uninitiated into the joys of bridge, be brought out of the darkness?

With Kramer's tennis circus as his model, Omar formed a bridge circus, enlisted stars of the first magnitude, and with a fanfare of trumpets, presented bridge as an exciting spectacle for the masses. Enthusiasts came to watch the exhibition matches. The masses stayed away and press coverage was subdued. To reach the public at large bridge had to break through to the television screen, and no man was better qualified to do it than Omar Sharif, the great film actor.

And so, on the eve of their departure for the States to do battle with the Aces, the stage was set in London for the greatest spectacle in the history of the game — a rubber bridge match for fabulous stakes against Crockfords, the oldest and most famous card club in the world.

The stakes were £1-a-point with heavy side-bets on every rubber. A syndicate backed the Crockfords standard-bearers, Jeremy Flint and Jonathan Cansino, Britain's best pair. Omar carried almost the entire amount himself.

What does £1-a-point represent? A comparative scale would show it to be 50 times higher than the big game at the Cavendish in New York or the St James's Bridge Club in London, about 2000 times higher than the average stakes in clubs on either side of the Atlantic, and 2400 times higher than the stakes in the celebrated game in Kansas City in 1929, when Mrs Bennet shot Mr Bennet dead after he had misplayed a 4♠ contract.

And yet, in this the biggest of all money matches, the money itself was the least important feature. To the players themselves it was little more than an irrelevancy. Omar had often played far, far higher at blackjack in Las Vegas, and at *chemin de fer* at Deauville. The exhorbitant stakes had been fixed for one purpose only — to capture the imagination of press and public, and so provide a dramatic setting for television. From the Rolls Royces at the entrance to the Piccadilly Hotel to the glamorous starlets selling programmes inside, television dominated every facet of the match and every thought of all who took part in it.

Interviewed on the eve of the match, Omar listed his hobbies as bridge, easily first, horses next and girls in third place, several lengths behind. This was no affectation. Bridge presented a challenge with every deal. Girls came too easily to rank high in importance.

> *Only yesterday over tea Baron Rothschild said to me*
> *I wonder, George, what it feels like to be poor*

Omar must have wondered at times what it felt like not to be chased by girls.

Some women, it is true, played bridge very well, notably world champion Fritzi Gordon. But Fritzi was no longer a girl and her daughter Nona, Omar's secretary at the time of the match, couldn't tell a smother play from a squeeze.

Omar's worst moment in the Piccadilly match came when he saw a bold front page headline in the *Daily Mail* proclaim: **Bridge Boob Costs Omar Sharif £1500.** He had stopped in a small slam when the critics, seeing all four hands, had courageously bid to seven.

Omar was furious. The critics were illiterate. Partner's responses on the precise Blue Club system showed that a king was missing and it might have been the king of trumps. What would the critics have said had he bid a grand slam on a finesse and gone down? He didn't mind bad reviews for his latest film. There was some justification for it. But that slam . . .

In the auditorium, filled to capacity, connoisseur spectators from home and overseas followed the play trick by trick, and watched the players themselves on closed-circuit TV monitors. Wilting under batteries of Kleig lights, perspiring but spellbound, every spectator was a participant.

In Omar's dressing-room during the dinner break only bridge was spoken, occasionally in French, more often in Italian. ". . . *l'Asso di fiori . . . distribuzione . . . malheureuse entame . . .*"

In marked contrast with the women of Dallas, the wives of the players were barely seen and never heard. Raymonde Delmouly, an emancipated French woman, went round with the wine. Maria-Luisa Garozzo and Antoinette Belladonna were not so presumptuous. None of them spoke English or knew much about bridge apparently, so they went shopping by day and were despatched to the ballet in the evenings. Shades of Dorothy and Betsy, Mary-Zita, Barbara and Judy!

It was a very different scene in the Crockfords camp. Jeremy and Jonathan dined alone or with their friend and manager, Irving Rose. Honor Flint, an international, many times a Life Master in American terms, kept studiously away during the breaks. The gladiators were not to be distracted. "No sex between sessions," said Irving Rose.

To complete the scheduled course of eighty rubbers, the last stage of the match was played in Omar's suite at the Mayfair Hotel. The Circus won by 5470 points. A few hours after a hilarious champagne and spaghetti party in the early hours of the morning, the Circus set off to America with high hopes of scoring the real victory, not against the Aces, but with them, in capturing the all-important television screen.

"What a good thing," observed Irving Rose, "that we had the foresight to form a company in Liechtenstein." Flint and Cansino had a 20 per cent interest in the film, and the tax advantage could run into five figures.

Who could tell that day that the film, with seemingly everything going for it, would prove a tragic and irretrievable flop?

Omar, who had invested £100,000, a quarter of a million dollars at the time, never got a penny back. He had done everything and given everything to make the film a success and, as the French say, *La plus belle fille du monde ne peut donner que ce qu'elle a*.

What went wrong?

According to the handful of prospective buyers who saw the film, and no one else did, the hastily installed air-conditioning interfered with the sound track. Some of the sequences were out of focus. Worse still, viewers had difficulty in seeing the cards as they were being played.

A leading film director and a leading producer had been engaged, but not a single scene had been rehearsed and crude technical faults, which could have been corrected had they come to light earlier, were perpetuated through every sequence.

Nine months after the match, with still no buyer in prospect, London's *Sunday Times* gave front-page prominence to a sensational report according to which Omar Sharif and his manager, Leon Yallouze, had been the victims of two adventurers who had formed a tin-pot company, contracted out the important work and enriched themselves carrying out the rest.

Omar took it philosophically. The loss of a quarter of a million dollars he treated with a disdain worthy of his spiritual ancestors in sixteenth-century Florence. No one had tried to film a bridge spectacle before, and pioneers couldn't expect to make a profit. He had no regrets. Neither did he feel he had been taken for a ride.

Leon Yallouze — 'when-ya-win Yallouze', said the *Sunday Times* — bore Omar's losses with the utmost stoicism.

Omar took up bridge during those frequent intervals on the set when an actor waits to be called. He once told an interviewer: "If I hadn't gone into films I would never have learned to play bridge, and that is probably the most important thing that's happened to me during my film career." He meant it.

The film-going public sees Omar as a great lover. Omar sees himself as a great bridge player. Is he?

Jean-Marc Roudinesco rates him as 'equal to the best'. Two hands, which I have picked as an example of different skills will, I believe, confirm Jean-Marc Roudinesco's judgement.

N/S vul: dealer South

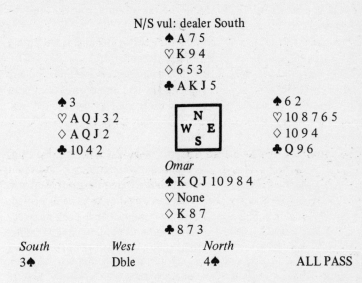

♠ A 7 5
♡ K 9 4
◇ 6 5 3
♣ A K J 5

♠ 3
♡ A Q J 3 2
◇ A Q J 2
♣ 10 4 2

♠ 6 2
♡ 10 8 7 6 5
◇ 10 9 4
♣ Q 9 6

Omar
♠ K Q J 10 9 8 4
♡ None
◇ K 8 7
♣ 8 7 3

South	*West*	*North*	
3♠	Dble	4♠	ALL PASS

A club was led and it looked to the kibitzers as if there was no way of avoiding four losers — a club and three diamonds. Omar had different ideas. Rising with dummy's ♣K, he ruffed a heart with the ♠8, carefully preserving the ♠4. Next a trump to the ace, another heart ruff, a high spade, removing the last adverse trump, and a club to the ♣A. Now came the key play, the ♡K on which Omar threw his last club. Whatever West did, one of declarer's four losers would disappear. Neither would it have mattered had the clubs broken 4-2, wherever the ♣Q might be.

Omar is declarer again in 4♠ in a regional tournament in Italy.

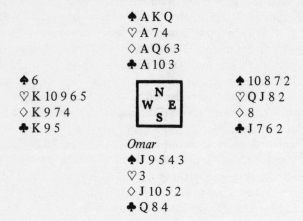

                    ♠ A K Q
                    ♡ A 7 4
                    ◇ A Q 6 3
                    ♣ A 10 3

♠ 6   ♠ 10 8 7 2
♡ K 10 9 6 5   N   ♡ Q J 8 2
◇ K 9 7 4   W   E   ◇ 8
♣ K 9 5   S   ♣ J 7 6 2

                    Omar
                    ♠ J 9 5 4 3
                    ♡ 3
                    ◇ J 10 5 2
                    ♣ Q 8 4

West led the ♠6. Omar played two more rounds of trumps, West discarding hearts. How could he get to his hand to draw the last trump? He couldn't afford to play the ♡A and ruff a heart, for he would then lose trump control before he had cleared the diamonds. A low diamond would do it so long as the suit didn't break 4-1. It did, and Omar wanted to allow for it.

The answer was as simple as it was imaginative. Omar led a *low* heart, away from the ♡A. Whatever the return, Omar could now afford to ruff a heart, draw the last trump and concede, if necessary, a diamond. With the ♡A still in dummy no harm could befall him.

In selecting Sharif hands there's an *embarras de richesse*, so many of his best plays and defences having been recorded.

> *When beggars die there are no comets seen*
> *The Heavens themselves proclaim the birth of Princes.*

As a Prince, Omar makes news where others wouldn't, but for all that there is no doubt that he is 'equal to the best'.

Both as a patron of the arts and as an artist himself, he has brought to bridge a new dimension, glamour — something it lacked in the headiest days of Culbertson. If he failed in his ambition to turn bridge into a spectator sport, he had blazed a trail for others who will surely reap where he has sown. Gradually, hesitantly, television is taking up bridge, solving one by one the technical problems which proved too complex for the Piccadilly film. Many more papers than ever before carry bridge features and some of them, on both sides of the Atlantic, bear the Sharif by-line. How many of his articles has Omar read? I wonder.

In *Return to Religion*, the American psychiatrist Henry C. Link, wrote: '. . . as a discipline in unselfish social habits and as a tonic for an able intellect, bridge ranks high in the category of worthwhile human activities'. This tonic Omar has dispensed with boundless energy and reckless generosity.

What of his hopes that bridge would play a part in improving human relations? Will people, in his words, play bridge and so have less time to hate each other? Not in the Middle East, alas, but on a far bigger stage, with still more momentous issues at stake, bridge has indeed played a part in the difficult dialogue between two worlds.

Across the aisle, facing Omar, Corn and Perroux, is the statue to Hsiao-yen, better known in the West as Katherine Wei. She looks tranquil and contented. She has good cause to be.

KATHIE WEI: EAST MEETS WEST

'In preparation for President Reagan's visit to China,' reported the *New York Times* in April 1984, 'bridge expert Kathie Wei was recently summoned to the White House to aid in briefing the President. Kathie Wei has had more direct contact with the top levels of the Chinese Government recently than almost any other American citizen.'

The detachment of a billion Chinese from the Soviet bloc has surely been the most momentous event since the Second World War. In the rapprochement with the West which followed, bridge has played a part far transcending in importance that of a mere game. For a star part in that performance destiny cast Yeng Hsiao-Yen, as she was born, Katherine Wei as she became, a bridge champion, whose remarkable personality and dual culture made her the ideal go-between.

To those untutored in the sorcery of dialectical materialism it may seem strange that bridge should play any part at all, symbolic or otherwise, in the conflict between world powers. Yet there is an unmistakable idealogical connection.

Just as the Puritans of old regarded cards as the play-things of the devil, so in the demonology of Marx and Lenin they are the playthings of the bourgeoisie — much the same thing, not as deadly as religion, of course, but still a form of 'opium for the people'.

If this makes no sense from this side of the great divide, it may be easier to grasp when seen from the other.

From the earliest days card-play in the Soviet Union was seen as a distraction from the class struggle and the coming world revolution, and therefore reprehensible. Trotsky and Torquemada would doubtless have looked upon bridge the same way, if not for the same reasons.

More than half a century ago Ely Culbertson described a visit to the Soviet State Card Trust. The Director showed him a graph indicating that sales had dropped by 40 per cent during the previous year. They had declined a further 20 per cent since. The visitor commiserated.

"You don't understand, Mr Culbertson," the Director told him. "Our production target is zero and with hard work we can achieve it."

Why then make cards at all? Because, explained the Director, a total ban on the manufacture of playing cards had led to a thriving black market in cards from Sweden. To counter it the authorities decided to create a State Card Trust which would freeze out the Swedes, then discourage the Russians by making the cards increasingly unattractive in quality and appearance.

Though bridge organisations are tolerated today in the Baltic States, there are none elsewhere in the Soviet Union. Bridge sections formed inside sports clubs exist, but are frowned upon. A resolution of the State Committee for Sport a few years ago deplored 'games which are harmful by running counter to the general course of social development'.

In Mao's China bridge was likewise regarded as a social evil. In a contemporary *Bulletin* the International Bridge Press Association reports the denunciation of Deng Xiaoping, soon to become China's strong man, during the Cultural Revolution. Not only was he charged with spending much of his time playing bridge, but also with favouring the careers of officials who were his cronies at the bridge table. The luxurious Cadres Club in Peking, 'built with stolen State funds', according to the *Red Guard Journal*, became Deng's bridge hangout, where he brought together 'capitulationists and renegades, demons and monsters'.

Now China is a member of the World Bridge Federation and on 24 October 1981 Deng Xiaoping accepted the Goren Award for the Bridge Personality of the Year. Unable to be present at the ceremony himself, Deng requested Mrs Katherine Wei to accept the award in his place.

For the Kremlin, China's blatant betrayal of the cause had sinister implications. A Moscow broadcast told the Soviet people that bridge is "extremely complex" and the ordinary Chinese know nothing about it. "But," said Moscow Radio, "the ruling clique is ready to play it for the West to be favourably disposed to help in strengthening military muscle."

How long before Kathie Wei emerges as a modern Basil Zaharoff, arms merchant *par excellence*?

Kathie sold no planes or tanks, but she helped to negotiate the first bulk shipment of American grain to China since 1949, and as Vice-President of her husband's Falcon Shipping Group she has been involved in many projects and investments on a multi-million dollar scale.

In 1980 Kathie was appointed adviser to the Shanghai Bridge League, and the same year she led the first American team to take part in the Shanghai International Bridge Tournament. She has visited China many times and has on several occasions played bridge with Deng himself.

In the *New York Times* Alan Truscott recalls the first occasion on which they played together. "What system shall we play?" asked Kathie. "Precision, of course," replied her host. Truscott records this deal in a friendly rubber in which Deng partnered Kathie, with Ding Guengen, his usual partner, sitting South.

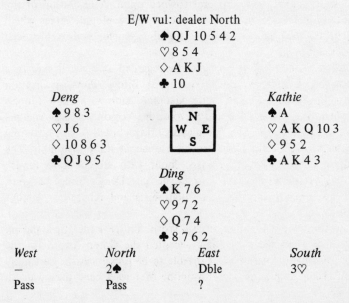

E/W vul: dealer North

                ♠ Q J 10 5 4 2
                ♡ 8 5 4
                ◇ A K J
                ♣ 10

Deng   Kathie
♠ 9 8 3   ♠ A
♡ J 6   ♡ A K Q 10 3
◇ 10 8 6 3   ◇ 9 5 2
♣ Q J 9 5   ♣ A K 4 3

                Ding
                ♠ K 7 6
                ♡ 9 7 2
                ◇ Q 7 4
                ♣ 8 7 6 2

West	North	East	South
—	2♠	Dble	3♡
Pass	Pass	?	

The 2♠ showed length but limited strength, and over Kathie's double Ding tried the time-honoured psyche, a bid in the other major to confuse the issue.

What should Kathie do when the bid came round to her? Double? That could be misunderstood. Even more so, 4♡. She passed and collected ten tricks in defence.

"You tried to bluff me, Mr Ding," said Deng. "Many men have tried to do that."

"And I succeeded, Mr Deng" replied Ding. "You could have made a vulnerable game in hearts."

"Now you are trying to bluff me again," rejoined the Vice-Chairman. "Had we bid game you would have called 4♠, would you not?"

"True," agreed Ding, "and you would have doubled, scoring the same 300, so I lost nothing."

"How about our 100 honours?" retorted Deng Ziaoping, accustomed to having the last word.

Bridge opened all the doors to Kathie Wei. And no one could have turned the magic key to such advantage. As Chinese as most Chinese, more American than most Americans, she is that very rare phenomenon, a completely bi-cultural being, as much at home with the ancient traditions and modern philosophy of China, as with the 'win, win, win' syndrome of American society. And win she has done, all along the line.

In *Second Daughter*, written in conjunction with Terry Quinn, she tells the story of her life, from early childhood in Peking, where her father, Professor Yang, was lecturer in sociology, through the turbulent years of the war and the revolution to what are surely her happiest days of all — the present.

The Japanese drove the family from Peking to take refuge in their ancestral home in Hunan, a thousand miles away and as many years behind in time. As the favourite grandchild of a feudal lord, with hundreds of retainers on his vast estate, she was taught by his third concubine, Fragrant Lotus, to grind ink and prepare pipes of opium. Her ambitious mother, whom she tried dutifully to love but couldn't bring herself to like, approved. It was bad for an eleven-year-old child to be woken in the middle of the night to prepare opium pipes, but being her grandfather's favourite was a big step on the road to success, and success was everything. Her mother, from whom Kathie has inherited her indomitable will, was proud of her daughter's gifts, yet bitterly ashamed of her birth. A mother in China was allowed one mistake, but if she gave birth to a second daughter it wasn't unusual to drown the child. Born in an enlightened Westernised *milieu* — her mother didn't even have bound feet, which profoundly shocked her aunt — Kathie was given the chance to atone for not being a boy.

From mediaeval Hunan the family followed the long trail to Chungking, seat of the Nationalist Government and a frequent target for Japanese air raids. Nothing could better illustrate Kathie's resourcefulness and strength of personality than an episode in that war-torn city, with no electricity, overrun by refugees, infested by rats. Her mother was gravely ill, wracked with fits of coughing, wasting away day by day. There were three hospitals in Chungking, but despite protective wire netting round the beds, rats posed a constant threat to the patients. Kathie's father called in a Dr Teng, 'shifty, ferret-faced', who diagnosed tuberculosis, holding out no hope of recovery.

Who could help? Only a Dr Li, German-trained specialist in diseases of the chest. He had a legendary reputation but, alas, he had lost both legs in a railway accident and now lived in seclusion on a mountain top, taking no patients. Kathie had heard about him from an American nurse at her school and from her, too, she learned of a Dr Lawson, once Dr Li's closest friend and colleague, who was now at the Baptist clinic in Chungking. For him, and for him alone, Dr Li might do a special favour.

Shouldn't he be approached? In vain Kathie pleaded with her father. The legless Dr Li couldn't move, he assured her, and even to seek his advice would make Dr Teng lose face — which was unthinkable.

Next morning, after her father left the house, Kathie put on her mother's finest dress — as dazzling as it was uncomfortable — and set out for the Baptist clinic, situated in the Valley of the Dying, the city's filthiest slum. As Professor Yang's daughter she gained access to Dr Lawson, explaining that her father, too ill to come himself, had sent her in his place. She wanted an introduction to Dr Li and would he, please, arrange for a jeep. Absurd, impossible request. Kathie, then fourteen, begged, cajoled, pleaded — until she got her way.

In Dr Li's aerie, a tumble-down ruin, Kathie's reception was frosty, but she wouldn't go away and just sat waiting for what seemed like eternity, hoping that the patience of the kindly American driver of the jeep, provided under protest by Dr Lawson, would not run out. The time came when her youth, her persistence and Dr Lawson's letter softened the cripple's heart and, carried in his wheel-chair with a medicine chest into the jeep, he was driven with Kathie to their home. The whole neighbourhood turned out to watch their arrival. There was a considerable American presence in Chungking and 'jeep girls' were not an uncommon sight. Kathie was put down as one of them, no doubt. She didn't care. She had brought the wizard to see her mother and that was all that mattered. He diagnosed pleurisy, administered the appropriate medicine – and her mother lived!

Would her father castigate or forgive her presumption? He never alluded to the subject, so she never found out.

The suffering she had witnessed in the Valley of the Dying, which she was to see again later in Shanghai, and the meeting with Dr Li, who worked such wonders, had deeply impressed Kathy. Increasingly, her thoughts turned to medicine as a career, and despite her mother's indignant protests – "touching their bodies, how could you!" – she decided to take up nursing.

No sooner was the war over than the Yangs moved to Shanghai, where her mother's family still lived in style. But Mao's Red Army was advancing fast and the days of the bourgeoisie were numbered. Just in time Kathie escaped to the United States, where within a year she had married Shen Chang-jiu, an eminently desirable suitor to whom her mother had betrothed her – a strictly unilateral match – while Shanghai was still safe.

Her first step on arrival in the States was to enrol at the Columbia University School of Nursing. After earning an advanced degree, she specialised at two hospitals, then worked her way up to be chief medical administrator at Kennedy Airport. She bore her husband three children. The second was a son, so there was no need to feel ashamed or to drown anyone.

A full life by any standard, but only the overture to the years that followed. After an amicable divorce, she married Chung'ching (Charles) Wei, millionaire ship-owner and bridge expert. Kathie took up the game in earnest, loved it and was determined, as in everything she did, to reach the top. She had the time, the money, the ability, and above all, the will to succeed.

With Benito Garozzo as her teacher it wasn't long before she was jousting with the best. By 1978 she had become a world champion, winning the Women's Pairs title at the Montreal Olympiad. A few years later her team won the Venice Cup, symbol of world supremacy for the stronger sex as the Bermuda Bowl is for men.

At bridge there were no more worlds left to conquer, but unlike Alexander the Great, she had no cause to feel frustrated, for beyond the card table there were other worlds where, allied to her many gifts, bridge proved to be more potent than the Macedonian phalanx. A catalyst, bringing diverse forces together, it was a language both East and

West could speak, though none so well as Hsiao-yen — Katherine Wei.

It is only fitting that the most popular system in China should be Precision, a truly Sino-American product, devised by Kathie's husband Charles.

Until 1969 no one had ever heard of it. Then, a team of gifted amateurs from Taiwan, coached by Charles Wei, came second in the world championship in Rio, beating into third place a star-studded American contingent. It was an astonishing performance and owed much to the inherent simplicity of Precision, which, in its original form, any bridge player could learn in half an hour.

Many players began to flock to the Precision standard. The Weis wanted there to be many more and promoted their brainchild by any and every means, regardless of cost. Precision players who won events of note received monetary rewards. Journalists and authors were encouraged to write about it. Inevitably, professionals took up the system, not because they thought it to be the best, but because it was undoubtedly the most lucrative. "Prostitution Club", sneered the critics but, day by day, the system made converts.

The latest super-charged model, incorporating sophisticated improvements inspired by Garozzo, is no longer so simple, but for everyday use there are less complex versions and these have swept the board in China. A British team which visited Peking in 1984 met no other.

Needless to say, Precision is the system Kathie Wei plays with her regular partner, Judy Radin, and their record speaks for itself.

Few today would think of Kathie as "the Winter Swallow", the pet name her opium-smoking grandfather gave her in Hunan. Her forceful ways and dominant personality do not endear her to everyone. "The Dragon Lady", her detractors call her, but what would they not give to change places!

As the heiress of two cultures, speaking the language and thinking the thoughts of both, Kathie has played a part on the world stage which no one else, man or woman, could have filled so well. Had Kipling met her, would he have written these lines?

> *East is East and West is West*
> *And never the twain shall meet.*

In Kathie Wei they have met, and the encounter has borne rich fruit.

"YOUR PEDESTAL AWAITS YOU, SIR"

As we leave the Pavilion of Eternal Life we come to an arresting sight, a pedestal waiting for a statue. From the other end of the aisle Culbertson seems to be looking at it expectantly.

Ely gave bridge an international language. Americans and Japanese, French, English, Germans, Italians all found in bridge a common tongue and a common bond.

What has happened to this great game today?

At the top, the universal language has been lost in a tower of Bable. The common bond has been dissolved in a plethora of systems and signals, cryptograms and codes, punctuated by alerts, protests and appeals. Bidding boxes and screens, shielding the players from a view of their partners, only serve to underline the ever-widening gulf between the masters at the summit of the pyramid and those below who play for fun, a vast, amorphous mass, growing bigger the world over, day by day.

How big is this mass?

Among the white races alone at least fifty million play the game. They belong mostly to the professional classes and the higher income groups, the most desirable target for sponsors and advertisers. Yet they stay away. Likewise the newsmen, the radio and television. Why?

Because by the nature of things it is the champions who bring the glamour and make the headlines, and today's champions, throwing smoke-screens at each other, are a bore.

When Culbertson did battle, millions the world over watched with bated breath. All were participants in a game played in the clear, which they could understand. All shared in the excitement.

Who could understand, or wish to understand, the game today, when Benito Garozzo himself, the most ingenious cryptographer of all, has to pull out of a match, as he did against the Danes in the Seattle Teams Olympiad in 1984, because — after the usual objections, protests and appeals — he was not allowed to keep his notes on the best defence against an incomprehensible system?

It's no surprise that the vicious circle spins faster and faster. As a counter to systems designed to confuse, the victims hit back in the same coin, making confusion worse confounded.

During Seattle the World Bridge Federation inaugurated a special telephone service with a number in Geneva reserved exclusively for relaying the latest scores from the Olympiad. Apparently, some hundred and fifty callers used the service daily. So far as press, radio and television were concerned, it was a case of "Sorry we've been troubled". In England, there were days when even the *Daily Telegraph* and *The Times* made no mention of the Olympiad, though both papers had correspondents on the spot.

With so conspicuous a void at the top, no Ira Corn or Omar Sharif can hope to break into television, turn bridge into a spectacle and capture the imagination of the public.

The World Bridge Federation, with no sense of purpose and a sense of direction to match, is chasing figures, measuring success by the number of countries and pseudo-countries it enrols as members, and becoming in the process increasingly politicised. Flouting both the letter and the spirit of its constitution, it has bowed to the demands of an unholy alliance of Third World and Communist Bloc countries to exile South Africa, pilloried for apartheid. The first act in elbowing out South Africa — where no colour bar of any kind has ever existed in bridge — was to stop an Indian and a Jew, the first pair to qualify, from representing South Africa in the Pairs Olympiad at Biarritz in 1982. What a blow against racial discrimination!

Israel has much the same enemies as South Africa, but unlike South Africa, she has powerful friends, so there is no question of driving her into exile. It is more expedient to arrange or rearrange the draw, to keep the Arabs and Israelis apart.

Not long ago any country which refused to play against another was suspended. Now the sails are trimmed according to the ill wind.

Can it be that the greatest indoor game in the world, a game that gives pleasure to so many millions and could give pleasure to so many more, will stay forever out of the public eye?

History teaches us that the occasion brings forth the man. Scanning the horizon, we look anxiously for signs of a new, reincarnated Culbertson to exorcise the evil spirits — the pygmies, the politicians, the cryptographs — and take bridge, *real* bridge to its rightful place in the scheme of things.

"Your pedestal awaits you, sir."

Index